The People's

Stanley Remembered

by

Alan Harrison & Jack Hair

This view of Station Road/Shield Row shows on the left, Railway Terrace with the Station Houses just below. On the right is Gordon Terrace and Rodham Terrace. Also in view is the old railway bridge at the lower end of the road.

Previous page: A Jazz Band at the lower end of Front Street before making their way up High Street in the 1960s.

Copyright © Alan Harrison and Jack Hair 1999

First published in 1999 by

The People's History Ltd.
Suite 1
Byron House
Seaham Grange Business Park
Seaham
Co. Durham
SR7 0PY

ISBN 1 902527 23 2

Contents

This view up Front Street from the 1960s shows St Joseph's School on the left, and on the right, going up the street are: Fine Fare, the Roma Cafe, Lloyds Electric Shop, Smaile's the dentists, a butchers and Swans, the Essoldo Cinema, Doggarts, Lloyds Bank and the Board School.

This is a similar view up Front Street in 1970, highlighting: the Wesleyan Church (centre left), the Co-Operative shops and tower (centre), Council Offices and other shops (right).

Introduction

As coal mining has played an important part of the history of Stanley and District for over 150 years, authors Alan and Jack have again included the subject in this their second book together. Other subjects covered are: Commerce, Religion, Around the Area, important local events and people of the district.

Both authors are conscious of bringing the history of the area up to date and it is hoped that by doing so, more people may be able to identify themselves and their families at work and, just as importantly, during their leisure time. Included are the usual collection of late nineteenth and early twentieth century photographs, plus, the 1940s, '50s, '60s and '70s.

Alan and Jack have mostly used information and pictures from their own collections, but they are grateful to the public who have also contributed.

This book has allowed them to cover local events such as, the Hedley Pit Heroes, the Bombs at Beamish, the Louisa Morrison Colliery Disaster, and a brief outline of the connection with Stanley and District, of Hillary Rodham Clinton, wife of the President of the United States of America.

The Essoldo Cinema, *circa* 1965. The Fine Fare supermarket, which opened in the autumn of 1961 is situated on the bottom left of the photograph – adjacent to the Roma Cafe. A 'Mr Whippy' ice cream van passes their fellow ice cream traders.

West Stanley campers during the 1926 General Strike.

Acknowledgements

The author's would like to thank:

Ritchie Hodgson, W.A. Benson (GP), Colin McPhail, Joan Callaway, Rita & Oreste Fella, Alan & Fred Westwater, George Nairn, George Mitchell, Ted Errington, Derek Hall, George Coates, Shirley Harrison, Raymond Soulsby, Margaret Anne Burrell, Tommy Hender, Eric Larmour, Pat McCue, Danny Fagan, Tissy Wright, Ralph Wilson, Beamish Photographic Archive and Carolyn Hall, Linda Varty, Anne Carr and the staff on Holmside Ward, South Moor Hospital, Chris Armstrong, Jim Robson, Oswald Barrass, the late Wm Brown, Mary Britton, Bob Drake, Chris Tarn, Brian Pears, Mary Murphy, Geoff Nicholson, Derek Jefferson, Jim Bradley, Joe Watson, Rev Richard Wallace, Ivan Garnham, Dominic Bove, Derwentside District Council (Environmental Health Dept), Durham County Council Records Office and all others who have helped in the production of this book.

Jack Hair, the son of a coal miner, was born in Joicey Square, Stanley in 1939. He attended Stanley Infant and Junior Schools and at 11 years of age went on to Annfield Plain Secondary Modern School. On leaving school, he had several jobs before settling for a career in the Civil Engineering Industry. He worked on projects throughout the country including bridge building on the M1 in the Bedfordshire and Buckinghamshire areas. He then worked mostly in the Durham, Cumberland and Westmoorland district and for many years on contract work for the Consett Steel Works. An injury at work forced him into early retirement. Jack was one of the founding members of Stanley Past and Present and was the founder member of South Moor Local History Group.

Alan Harrison was born in 1951 and has resided in Stanley for most of his life. He attended St Mary's R.C. School at Hustledown then Towneley R.C. Secondary Modern until the age of 16. Upon leaving school he had several jobs, including working in the Steel Works, a battery factory, on the oil rigs and a hospital porter; before commencing nurse training in 1991 and subsequently qualifying as a RGN in 1994. Alan was a member of the Stanley Past and Present group and is a member of South Moor Local History Group.

AROUND THE AREA

This early 1960s view up the High Street shows, on the left, the Stanley Inn, the Tin School, St Andrew's Institute, the Pavilion Cinema, the Northern Club and the Drill Hall. On the right are the shops at the Elite Buildings, the Gas Board Shop, the Police Station and the Salvation Army Citadel. Most of the buildings have now been demolished in the name of progress.

Front Street, Stanley, *circa* 1910. A view looking down the street with James Sword (photographers) on the immediate right and Slater and Costelloe (pawnbrokers) adjacent.

Front Street, Stanley, *circa* 1925. A view looking up the street with the Queen's Hotel (built in 1898) on the immediate right. Note the increase in traffic from the previous photograph.

Two views of well-known 'corners' of Stanley Front Street in 1964. The first shows a rainy day in the town, the camera pointing up the street and capturing 'Jackson's Corner', named after the tailors which opened there in 1938. A little further up stood Westwater's Confectioners and Tobacconists, and Woolworths who have occupied the same site since 1955. The two ladies on the crossing may be heading for Broughs Store which stood just off the photograph to the right. The second view shows, to the right, 'Dodgson's Corner', named after the newsagents which stood there for many years. Timothy White, the chemist, is adjacent and Lloyds Bank is situated in the same premises they occupy today.

Stanley Front Street, *circa* 1890. This is one of the oldest views of Stanley. On the left, going down the street, the houses and shops shown are now the TSB and the Empire Club, followed by Cromarty House, the Commercial Inn and Havanah House. The large trees in the background were in fact an orchard belonging to Havanah House, later the site of the Board School. Next to that is St Andrew's and on the right are an assortment of small shops and houses and the original Wesleyan Methodist Chapel. Note there were no raised footpaths.

Juvenile Jazz Bands, *circa* 1963. During the 1960s, '70s and '80s, juvenile marching bands were popular throughout Durham with most towns and villages having their own band. This band is coming down Front Street on the way to Murray Park.

Oxhill Central Workingmen's Club

The club is known locally as 'The Arch' from the girder bridge that once spanned the entrance to Park Road. The site was previously an allotment garden and the premises, when first built, served as an undertakers' shop. The proprietor was Mr W. Turner.

August 1958 saw the official re-opening of the club after £6,000 worth of improvements. The club's oldest member at that time – George Clarke – performed the opening ceremony. He told onlookers that he had first attended the club in 1898, though it was not affiliated to the Club Union until 1907.

The girder bridge was removed in 1964 and, with the subsequent levelling of the railway embankment, the club today occupies a prominent position adjacent to a busy road junction.

The club is on the right with the road leading under the bridge to South Moor.

Right: A view of the bridge from the South Moor side – Joicey Terrace is visible through the opening.

A club outing from 1930. Included are: Joe Bowman, Billy Brown, Tommy Thompson, Jack Errington, Joe Burt, Billy Cattle, Billy Shields, Tom Ivey, Arthur Nichol and Blind Joe Bulman (4th from right – front row).

Holmside and South Moor Miners' Welfare Fund Hospital

This hospital is very highly regarded by the local community, mostly in the knowledge that it was built for the miners and their families out of the fund set up solely for their welfare by order of the Mining Act of 1920. The money for the building of this hospital was raised by a levy of one penny on every ton mined in every year in that particular area – paid by the coal owners to the welfare fund. Once constructed, the hospital was financed by weekly off-takes from the miners' wages. The fund could not be used for other purposes than the welfare of the workers and their families. The principle of the fund was to improve the life of the community.

The first serious suggestion for a local hospital was made in 1884 by Messrs Mark Archer and James Fairley. They were unable to raise the money privately and the plan was dropped.

A hospital was again suggested by Coroner Graham in February 1909 at the inquest into the Burns Pit Disaster held in St Andrew's Institute, Stanley. Coroner Graham was appalled to find injured survivors were compelled to lie amongst the dead bodies for lack of a proper place. The make-shift hospital reeked of death.

In 1913, plans for a hospital were actually drawn up. The proposed site was just south of the Miners' Rescue Station at Hustledown. Once again lack of finance delayed any progress.

In 1920, the Mining Act was passed compelling the coal owners of the country to set up a fund solely for the benefit and welfare of the miners and their dependants. In those times the life of the working man was very hard and this was seen as a great step forward for them.

A committee was set up in Durham composed of representatives from the Coal Owners and the Durham Miners' Association whose principle was to formulate ideas for miners' welfare. They pushed forward the idea of a hospital.

By mid 1923 progress was so good that on the 24th September 1923, Coal Owners and Miners' Associations decided to appoint officers to administer the business of building a hospital. Mr T. Greener was appointed Chairman.

An aerial view of the hospital in 1947. The Miners' Rescue Station is to the right with St Mary's R.C. School directly below and St Mary's R.C. Church to the left of the school.

However, it was decided that funds would not be released until it was sure that the proposed hospital could be self financing after construction and this created a great burden on the miners' off-takes.

Estimates of the yearly cost per bed was £90-£100, but as the local doctors had offered their services free of charge, the estimated cost per bed was reduced to £80 per annum. The total yearly cost on the 26 bed accommodation was £2,080.

The Main Ward with 12 beds which was opened in 1927. It is now the Hedley Rehabilitation Unit.

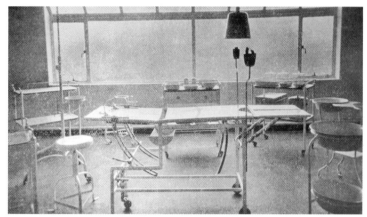

The Operating Theatre upon opening. It is now a three bedded men's ward.

It was estimated that one penny per miner per week would return £1,820 per annum, leaving a substantial deficiency. On the 10th November 1923, Mr Cooper of South Moor Coal Co. informed Mr Greener that the coal owners were prepared to donate a sum not exceeding £1,000 per annum plus the gift of five acres of land for the hospital site. But for these gifts, the hospital scheme would have been much less elaborate.

Mr T. Milburn was appointed to organise a competition by architects to design a new hospital. The winner would get £75, the second £50, and the third £25. In all, 75 designs were submitted and an award was made on 5th April 1924. First prize went to Messrs Buckland & Heywood of Birmingham and they were duly appointed to design the hospital. Messrs Thomas Lumsden, building contractors from Newcastle were awarded the contract and work commenced in March 1925. The hospital was completed in July 1926 on schedule.

The building was to accommodate twenty-eight adults and six children in four wards. Two male wards, one female ward, and one children's' ward, with the addition of two single-bed wards.

The great day that everyone had strived for finally arrived. The opening day was on 29th January 1927. South Moor Colliery Band led a large parade headed by the Lodge Banner to the hospital. Mr Robson of the Durham Miners' Association performed the opening ceremony. The vicar of Craghead, the

Rev J. Eddon offered prayers at the commencement of the ceremony and dedicated the building.

On behalf of the Hospital Committee, it was stated:

The good ship is launched,
She is thoroughly
seaworthy,
It now depends on the
navigators,
To bring her safely through,
All the storms of stress and
weather.

Despite threatened closure in the early 1990s, the hospital continues to thrive to the present day. It offers out-patient services to the people of the area, along with the 20 bedded Holmside Ward providing in-patient rehabilitation for patients recovering from operations or injury.

Ward Manager, Carolyn Hall (left) and In-Patient Manager, Maureen Harrison collecting the award for Quality Care from Cabinet Minister, Jack Cunningham in London in January 1999.

Staff on the present Holmside Ward who achieved the relatively rare distinction of retaining their Charter Mark. Back row, left to right: Alistair Rodda, Anne Forster, Marie Newton, Catherine Roberts, Maureen Harrison, Shirley Walton. Middle row: Gloria Barron,

Caroline Deacon, Margaret Ivison, Margaret Guest, Dorothy Smith. Front row: Anne Carr, Pamela Richards, Carolyn Hall.

Life On The Wards

Prior to becoming a staff nurse, and then a sister at South Moor Hospital in the early 1960s, I trained as a State Registered Nurse and a midwife. I had trained at the Royal Victoria Infirmary, Princess Mary's and Newcastle General, and worked as a midwife at Richard Murray Hospital.

At South Moor I worked on wards 4 and 3, nursing patients who were convalescing from heart or lung surgery or who on week days travelled to Newcastle General Hospital for radiotherapy – some being allowed home at weekends. These wards later became general and orthopaedic surgery, with operations being performed three days each week.

I then worked as a sister alongside Sister Sample on both of these wards and in theatre. We were assisted by staff nurses, enrolled and auxiliary nurses, some came from Lee Hill and Maiden Law hospitals for training. The nursing staff worked spilt duties commencing at 7.30 am and finishing at 5 pm or 8 pm, after having three hours off duty during the day. We had one and a half days off each week. On the wards, duties were allocated to nurses both morning and afternoon. Help was given with the morning ward cleaning and patients' meals. Syringes, needles and instruments were cleaned and sterilised, and dressings and swabs made by the nurses, dressing drums filled and these were sterilised by the porters. Patients on sunny days were allowed to sit outside or stroll in the gardens, assisted by the nurses when necessary.

Joan Callaway

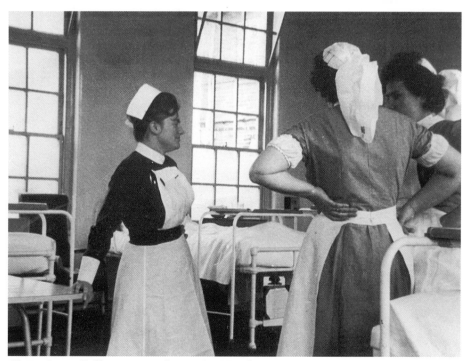

Sister Joan Callaway on the Main Ward.

These four photographs formed part of a survey undertaken by North Eastern Railways in 1921, of level crossings on the line between Chester-le-Street and Annfield Plain.

The level crossing at Oxhill looking along the road leading into Stanley. On the left is the Ox Inn and on the immediate right is Oxhill Methodist Chapel.

This is the opposite view to the photograph above, looking along to New Kyo. The railway signal box is on the left.

The level crossing leading into the Louisa Colliery – the road leading into Stanley. A saddle tank locomotive is on the track from West Shield Row Colliery which was sunk in 1854 by Charles Edward Oakey and became known as 'Oakey's Pit'. It closed for a while then re-opened in 1869 when the Dickenson family took it over and it became West Shield Row Colliery. It was subsequently taken over by the South Derwent Coal Company. Coals were drawn and taken to Stanley in tubs by rope haulage to the screening plant which stood opposite the Louisa Pit. The loading wagons were taken over the level crossings, known locally as Dickenson's Crossings, first by horses and later by locomotive to the mineral line. Empty wagons were brought back on the return journey. West Shield Colliery closed in November 1934 and the level crossings fell into disuse and were eventually removed.

The opposite view to above, looking to Oxhill. The level crossing gates to the right are closed. This was adjacent to Louisa Terrace.

Stanley Board School, pre summer holidays, 1930. Included in the photograph are: J. Drummond, C. Herdman, Bill Falgate, L. Kingston, Jim Allison, Miles Armstrong, Bob Fenwick, Ted Henderson, Eddie Soulsby, Joe Nicholson, Tommy Telford, Maurice Metcalfe, Joe Carr.

West Kyo Board School, 1918. In the middle row are: Meggie Speed (2nd from right), Nellie Speed (3rd from right) and Johnina Speed (4th from right).

Hammels Diamond Bus – an old Bedford bus, Reg No JNN 656 which ran from Stanley to Quaking Houses. It is at the bus stand outside the Co-Operative Boot & Shoe Department at the top of Front Street, Stanley. There was great competition between the Diamond Bus Company and the Northern Bus Company, both on

this route and the Stanley to Durham Service. The Diamond still operate but are now owned by the Northern.

Hunters bus.

Hunters of Tantobie have traded as a bus company and road haulage business since motor vehicles first came into the area, and even before that with horse drawn vehicles. They and other independent operators united to compete with Northern on the Stanley to Flint Hill route via Tantobie.'

In more recent years, only Hunters and Holmes remained of the independents, but now only Hunters still cover this public service route, plus operating private hire coaches and their road haulage business from the Tantobie Garage.

Hunters lorry at depot.

A selection of Chisholm's early buses and drivers. Chisholm's buses from Craghead were part of a group of independent bus companies who traded for many years as 'Diamond'. Chisholm's was based at Craghead behind the Punch Bowl.

John Tyman standing next to Northern Bus Reg No CU 4500 in the 1950s. All bus companies used to park up in Scott Street while they were off service. Scott Street was also used as a destination turning point. Note the old houses in the background. They were situated in the area known as the 'Isle of Man' with street names such as Douglas, Ramsey, Peel and Forster.

Gas House Square

This area of housing was to the south of Stanley High Street at the end of Bell and Beaconsfield Streets. They were built for the coal miners of the Burns Pit. Originally, the upstairs bedrooms were only accessible by ladder but some modernisation later took place. They had ash midden type toilets which were later updated. The streets were Rifle, Kettledrum and Henry. They also included Agnes Street. These houses were adjacent to the local gas works which were erected by the Burns and later taken over by the Northern Gas Board. There were also coal hoppers next to the houses.

Right: Billy Watson and his nephew Phil in Rifle Street in the late 1930s.

Left: The demolition in the 1950s of Henry Street. The photograph was taken from the coal hoppers.

Right: Agnes Street. This short street still remains and is part of the Diamond Bus Depot and Offices. The garage and houses are situated at the road turn just opposite St Andrew's Institute. In 1909, hardly a house in Gas House Square escaped losing a male member of their family in the Burns Pit Disaster.

Mary Ruddick in the back street of Joicey Terrace with Oxhill School in the background. Mary and her husband John now run a successful electric business in Tyne Road.

Joicey Terrace being demolished.

Syd Wears snr, the High Street butcher used to rear his own pigs in a garden not far from his home near the King's Head. These animals, once fattened, were slaughtered by Syd for the shop. His daughter, Lestryne, is pictured visiting the animals and, by the size of them, they will soon be getting a visit from Syd.

Old East Stanley (The Lanes)

East Stanley was known locally for many years as 'The Lanes'. The terrace houses and bungalows were mostly built for coal miners and their families and many large families were brought up in these houses.

A general view of Noel Street.

The village was almost self contained with all the necessary facilities for day to day life; such as a school, post office, Methodist Church and Church of England Mission Hall, ambulance station, reservoir, workingmen's club, Women's Institute, garage and filling station, Co-Op Branch, newsagents, fish and chip shop and several general dealers. There was also the Welfare Sports Ground for cricket, football, tennis and other activities; and also allotment gardens.

A selection of some of those old streets were:

The VG Foodstore and East Stanley Workingmen's Club, Noel Street.

East Street, built 1897.
West and Far West Street, built in 1893 for Joicey.
Chester Road, built 1902/03 and a further 17 houses and a shop in 1910.
Noel Street, built in 1905.
Cecil Street, built in 1909/11 and a further 4 houses in 1925/26.
Ann Street, built in 1905.
Sand Street, built in 1913.
John Wilson Aged Miners' Cottages, built in 1914.

Most of these houses are long gone and replaced with council houses and bungalows. Those who lived there speak of 'The Lanes' with great affection.

Slater's newsagents shop, Chester Road with School House on the right.

West Street under demolition.

The fish and chip shop, Chester Road.

A view of Chester Road along to Stanley.

Most workingmen's clubs had women's sections known as 'The Jolly Girls'. They held weekly meetings and sometimes did exchange visits to other clubs to give concerts. This group, in East Stanley Club, include: Evelyn Stephenson, Isabel Hair, Mary Marley, Kitty Dover and Lily Cutherbertson, the remaining names are not known

Kyo Lane Uproar Band. Little is known of this group or the date but they are obviously dressed up for the occasion.

Stan Coates on the accordion and Nutty Kendall on the drums at Burnhope in 1946. They played at local events and dances throughout the area in the 1940s.

Stanley Park (View Lane)

Stanley Park (View Lane). This land was originally part of Shield Row Woods owned by Slingsby D. Shafto. Around 1899 the site was offered to Stanley Council for use as a park at £10 annual rent. This was turned down. However, by 1914 plans for a park were submitted with estimated building work costs of £2,400 and purchase price of over £1,000 for an area of seven acres (537 square yards). By 1925 a surrounding wall was erected using stone from the site. In 1928 Hunter Miller gifted wrought iron gates from Mayo House on Shield Row Bank. In 1926 a loan of £3,000 was sought for the completion of the park. However, for lack of funds, the park stayed as it was for several years until Parks Supt. John Tyerman took up the task in 1929 and made a grand job laying out the park. Lawns, flower beds and walking areas were laid out with additions over the years. Public toilets, and other small buildings, followed by the bowling green and putting green which were opened on the 26th May 1931 with a bowls match between councillors and council office staff. The park continued to make progress with regular brass band contests. An aged persons' shelter was built and the tennis courts were opened in 1934. A tennis pavilion was erected in 1946. Around this time, a children's recreation area was opened in the east end of the park. This was a pleasant park well stocked and laid out and tendered by the park keeper. However, in the 1980s this all ended to save costs. The park gates were removed, the surrounding fence taken down and the park keeper no longer based in the park full time. This may have saved costs but the cost to the public for the loss of a once beautiful facility was too great and it soon went downhill. The gifted gates were not replaced and may even be lost. Vandals roam freely into the park spoiling the bowling green, the only remaining facility. However, efforts are in place to help save the park by interested local people.

West Road, Annfield Plain. In the foreground are a group of men standing around the entrance to the underground toilets, probably waiting for the pubs to open. These toilets were strangely sited in the middle of the road. They were opened in 1907 and demolished in 1917.

Albert Harrison and family dogs, Billy and Tinker in Towneley Street, *circa* 1949. Albert was tragically killed in an accident at the Louisa Pit in 1951. Note the gas works tower in the distance.

COMMERCE

Thomas Bainbridge, a local butcher from Catchgate.

The firm of W. Pinkham & Son Ltd (Glove Manufacturer) began in Devon in 1899. In 1901 the family moved to Witham in Essex; the business expanded and in 1912 they built a factory. Foreign competition forced the company to close down in 1929, but the business was soon restarted and by 1939, it was firmly established. In 1948 a modern factory was built at Witham, and a factory was opened at South Moor – above the Co-Operative Hall. Finally, in 1959, a new modern factory was opened in Anthony Street, Stanley. The premises is today owned by Ashtons (Manufacturing) Ltd.

W. Pinkham & Son Ltd, South Moor.

W. Pinkham & Son Ltd, Stanley.

These are two photographs linked by family ties. *Above*: P. Kaiser's business in Tyne Road, 21st October 1954. Following a lifetime in the mines, he began his catering business in 1954 and his wife extended it to provisions and home bakeries. *Below*: Oxhill Service Station, 12th November 1959. The proprietor was Michael Kaiser, only son of P. Kaiser. He went into business in May 1959 – three months before his 16th birthday with his parents acting as guarantors.

This property was owned by my grandparents, Mr and Mrs Elliott and was situated in Brewery Square. Two of their daughters managed the business. Olive served in the shop which was a general dealers and home bakery. Rose did the baking which consisted of bread, tea, cakes, fruit tarts, cakes and meat pies – this meant a very early start for her

W.R. Elliott's shop. Mr Elliott is standing in the doorway with his wife Margaret Ann and daughter Olive.

every day, except Sunday when the shop was closed. There was a great demand for the products and many of the customers placed regular orders for bread, etc. Saturday morning was always a very busy time, as people bought extra for the weekend. The shop was open from 8.30 am to 6 pm. My mother Emma, who was the oldest daughter, worked in the shop until 1923 when we moved to Dunston as dad was promoted from Stanley to Bensham Depot of the Northern Bus Company. After the death of my grandparents, the business was sold in the early 1950s.

Margaret Anne Burrell

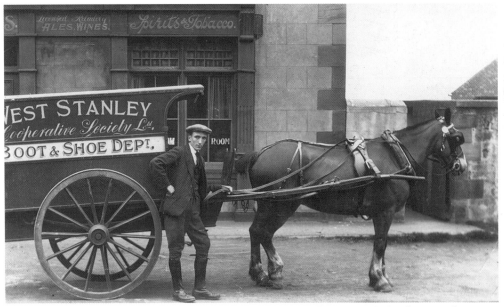

Wilfred Robson with 'store' horse and cart out on his rounds in the Stanley area, *circa* 1930. His daughter, Cynthia, also worked for the Co-Op and was for a time at the East Stanley Branch. She is now a supervisor at the Asda Superstore in Stanley.

Margaret Ann 'Nye' Wilson, surrounded by her family of nine daughters: Nellie, Georgina, Ada, Sally, Eva, Peggy, Maimy, Lena and Jean. The family had a general dealers at 88 Pine Street, South Moor for many years, beginning just after the First World War. In the late 1920s they also commenced business at 58 School Terrace, South Moor; the running of these premises finally being left to daughter Nellie and her husband William Sydney Lumley. When Nellie opened a wool shop just around the corner on Park Road, John Dixon took over the shop around 1950. The Dixons sold the business to Jack and Winnie Young, who took over the shop on the 15th August 1960, and Jack still runs the shop to this day.

The photograph was taken around 1932 at Sally's wedding. Peggy married Albert Graham and their son Benny is today a well known folk singer along with Bob Fox. Lena's son, Harry Hender, boxed for the NCB at Welterweight in the 1950s. Eva's son Billy Lonsdale was a drummer in several big dance bands, playing in London and on Ocean Liners.

Right: Fred Wright with his ice cream cart, South Moor, 1936.

Roma Cafe

Angelo Fella began an ice cream business in Italy before moving to Paris with his wife Giuditta. Whilst in the French capital their daughter Celestina was born in 1897 and when the little girl was six they moved to Glasgow to an ice cream shop near Ibrox Park.

The cold north eventually defeated Angelo's dreams of success however and on doctor's advice he returned to his hometown of Valvori in Italy. It was in Valvori in 1921, at the little local church of Our Lady of Sorrow, that Celestina married Cesare Niro, later known as 'Charlie' to the people of Stanley.

The couple moved to England in 1922 and formed a partnership with Celestina's sister Stella

Charlie Niro, standing in the shop doorway in August 1951.

Dimascio in an ice cream shop in Spennymoor. Finally in 1927 Charlie and Celestina moved into their own premises in 9 Front Street, Stanley and opened the Roma Cafe. The previous occupant had been Alfred Boothroyd the optician. Several years later the business was expanded when they took over the adjoining premises of 11 Front Street, previously occupied by the Maypole Dairy Co. Ltd.

The Roma Cafe, in the early days, with 'Charlie' Niro standing in the doorway. Further down the street are the premises of the Stanley & District Gas Company, Thomas Scanlan (outfitters) and William Robson (butcher). The premises of Johnson Brothers (Dyers) Ltd stand on the end of Station Road.

Daughter Rita Maria was born in Stanley and in 1957 she married Oreste Fella at St Joseph's Church. Rita's father, Charlie, sadly died a year later but her mother Celestina lived on until 1990, actually seeing the end of her business in Front Street. The family left the shop in August 1988 to concentrate on manufacturing and delivering their ice cream to customers via their fleet of vans.

Rita at the wheel of one of the early vans used by the Roma Cafe to sell their ice cream around the streets of Stanley District.

A Popular Meeting Place

The shop opened in 1927 and in the early days was open seven days a week closing at 11 pm – there were eleven staff at that time. The hours were then changed to 9 am to 9.30 pm – the closing time was later changed to 7.30 pm with the shop closed all day Wednesday. Dad died in 1958 aged 57. The shop was sold on 19th August 1988 but vans still sell ice cream locally. Mam died at 93 and still came into the shop until it closed – she enjoyed seeing the customers.

Rita Fella

The premises in May 1951. On the right in the doorway is Rita Niro. On the left, just inside the shop is mother, Celestina.

Above & right: The Roma Cafe as many people will remember it in the 1960s - these photos were taken in 1961.

Oreste and Rita receiving 1st Prize of the Silver Challenge Cup in 1966 at Blackpool.

Ice Cream Award

We won several national awards. The first major award we won was the first prize for the Silver Challenge Cup at Blackpool in 1966. In 1971 we won the second prize, Silver Medal at Scarborough. Two years later we won a Diploma of Merit at the Expo CT International Exhibition in Milan. In 1991 another award was won in Verona – a Special Diploma and Gold Medal. As well as these awards, over the years, we won a number of Special Diplomas and Diplomas of Merit.

Rita Fella

Westwater Family

The Westwater family began in business in Spennymoor in the 1870s selling fruit and sweets from their shop. James Westwater, a wholesale leather merchant, came to Stanley in 1897 and opened a leather work shop and fruit shop in Front Street. The family were strong Wesleyan Methodists and James was a local preacher.

Andrew Westwater was born in 1894. On the death of his mother in 1897 his grandmother in Spennymoor raised him until 16 years of age, by which time his father had remarried, and Andrew returned to Stanley. The family business had by now primarily become confectionery and tobacco. Andrew served in the First World War, joining the Tyneside Scottish in 1915, becoming a Sergeant and was wounded three times. On return to civilian life he and his father opened a sweet factory in Stanley in 1921 near to where the police station is today; eventually supplying many shops in County Durham and Tyneside. However, the general strike and subsequent depression caused the Westwater family to abandon their excursion into sweet manufacturing.

In 1927 they bought a shop, gradually acquiring more until 1935 when the father and son partnership was dissolved. James retired and Andrew assumed control of the four shops. These were located in High Street (near the Pavilion Cinema), 62 Front Street (near Woolworths), 216 Park Road (near South Moor Hotel) and West Road, Annfield Plain.

Andrew served as a special constable in the Second World War and was also appointed as emergency food officer for Stanley, Consett and Chester-le-Street in case of enemy invasion. He was a member and trustee of Oxhill Methodist

Westwater's Shop, Front Street, Stanley. On the left is Miss Mollie White, manager of the shop for 46 years. On the right is Andrew Westwater.

The National Union of Retail Confectioners Dinner, circa 1958. In the centre is Andrew Westwater and his wife. On the right is Billy Grant and his wife (from Craghead Post Office).

Church and was a keen supporter of the Boys Brigade. In 1948 he founded the North West Durham Branch of the National Union of Retail Confectioners and became its first president, later becoming national president.

Andrew had three children Joan, Fred and Alan. Eldest son Fred was trained in retail confectionery and tobacco in Newcastle and eventually managed the four shops on the death of his father and mother who both died in 1965. Later, two additional shops were added, one at Dipton and one at New Kyo.

Youngest son Alan, who had qualified as a P.E. teacher, took over the running of the retail shops in 1974 when Fred left to become a teacher at Tanfield Comprehensive School. Fred eventually retired in 1998. Alan served for several years as a councillor for South Moor Ward, and formed Oxhill Youth Club in the early 1960s.

The Westwater retail business suffered considerably with the opening of the Stanley by-pass road in 1974. Their High Street shop was demolished for the re-development, and the Front Street shop suffered due to the buses being re-located behind Front Street. Many passengers on their way to and from work had popped into Westwaters for cigarettes, sweets etc, and nearly all this trade was now lost.

Eventually the family wound up their businesses and by the early 1980s the name Westwater no longer appeared amongst the shops of Stanley and District.

Andrew Westwater in Police Uniform at Oxhill in 1944 with his two sons, Alan, on the left, and Fred.

Walter Willson's staff, Stanley, 1945. The Walter Willson's grocery chain was founded in 1875, with a shop at Bishop Auckland, by Walter de Lancey Willson and his partner Stephen Aitchison. By 1953, the firm had 193 stores mainly in pit villages. It was taken over in 1998 by the Southampton-based firm Alldays. In the photograph are, back row: Barbara Bartle, Betty Murphy, Florence Dempsey. Front row: Edith Coxon, Joyce Brown, Florence Pringle (manageress).

Right: Walter Willson's, Craghead.

Below: Walter Willson's, Burnopfield.

Furnishing a Comfortable Home *without a large initial outlay* **AND PAY OUT OF INCOME!**

S. HODDER,
MAIN ST. SOUTH MOOR.

If you don't see what you require in the window! Ask for it, we can get it!

An advertisement for S. 'Cosh' Hodder, *circa* 1930. His shop stood opposite to where Millers was situated. They also sold gramophones and pianos.

The exterior of South Moor Meadow Diary. The young boy on the left is Matt Stoker, aged 14.

J.E. Temple's butchers shop, Tantobie.

Theatre Royal Advert Postcards.

An advertisement for the Theatre Royal.

An advertisement for a stage production of 'Napoleon' at the Theatre Royal.

Peter Duffy, M.M.

Modern Magician and Illusionist.

10, RITSON STREET, STANLEY,
Co. DURHAM.

Peter Duffy's personalised card.

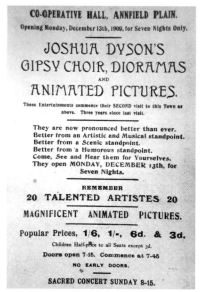

CO-OPERATIVE HALL, ANNFIELD PLAIN.

Opening Monday, December 13th, 1909, for Seven Nights Only.

**JOSHUA DYSON'S
GIPSY CHOIR, DIORAMAS
AND
ANIMATED PICTURES.**

These Entertainments commence their SECOND visit to this Town as above. Three years since last visit.

They are now pronounced better than ever.
Better from an Artistic and Musical standpoint.
Better from a Scenic standpoint.
Better from a Humorous standpoint.
Come, See and Hear them for Yourselves.
They open MONDAY, DECEMBER 13th, for
Seven Nights.

REMEMBER
20 TALENTED ARTISTES 20

MAGNIFICENT ANIMATED PICTURES.

Popular Prices, 1/6, 1/-, 6d. & 3d.

Children Half-price to all Seats except 3d.

Doors open 7-15. Commence at 7-45
NO EARLY DOORS.

SACRED CONCERT SUNDAY 8-15.

An advertisement for Joshua Dyson's
Gypsy Choir, Dioramas and Animated
Pictures at the Co-Operative Hall,
Annfield Plain. As stated in the advert, the
show previously visited the town in 1906.

An advertisement for the final film
shown at the Pavilion Cinema –
Godzilla Versus The Thing. Shortly
afterwards the cinema converted
over to Bingo.

An advertisement for the Victoria
Theatre featuring principle actress,
Miss A. Harrison Tate.

The Cinemas Of Stanley: A Personal Record By George Coates

George began work as a projectionist in the Odeon Cinema, Newcastle in 1953. He moved to the Essoldo, Stanley in 1954 and stayed until 1958 when he joined the RAF. Leaving the RAF in 1961 he worked at the ABC-REX, Consett until 1963 when he returned to the Essoldo. He finally left in 1970 to join Western Electric Group Systems. George is still involved in the cinema business today – travelling around the North of England and Scotland maintaining the sound systems.

The Auditorium of the Essoldo, 1954.

The Classic group had taken over the Essoldo in 1970 and by 1976 it had closed. The projectionist in its final years was Malcolm Collins. After standing derelict for many years the premises has recently been demolished with the intention of turning the area over to residential accommodation.

George Coates took all of the following photographs of the Stanley Cinemas with the exception of the Foyer of the Essoldo and the Pavilion orchestra.

The Essoldo Cinema, 1954.

A view of the lower part of Front Street and the top of Church Bank and Station Road, taken from the roof of the Essoldo in 1954. The Stanley Inn, 'Paddy Rocks', public house is prominent on the corner.

Foyer of Essoldo Cinema - Bob Mitchell - Commissionaire. Vera Tuckermann (née Woods) – Cinema Usherette.

Albert Hall

The building was built by Richard Murray, landlord of the Commercial Hotel, on land belonging to Mr Davison, a cowkeeper. It opened as the Royal Theatre, 14 days before the Victoria Theatre, in June 1893, and closed after three months. Upon re-opening the name was changed to the Albert Hall, after Queen Victoria's husband Prince Albert.

The Albert was a plain stone building inside and out with the stage standing at the East End. The entrance comprised of two pairs of large double doors at the West End. A large cellar was used as a lodging house in the early days; the entrance being on the North side. The building had many uses before conversion to cinema, including: drill hall, dances, balls, bazaars, boxing, sales and variety shows.

The first public building in Stanley to give all pictures shows was the Co-op Hall, which stood at the top of Stanley Front Street. It was leased by Wallaw Picture Co. in 1908 and admission was 3d and 6d.

Randell Williams took over the Albert Hall in 1910 and converted it into a cinema; enlarging the premises by constructing a new stage at the East End, and a new entrance at the front, providing a gallery. Early programmes read 'Randell Williams Picture Hall' – resident Manager George E. Routledge.

The Albert Hall closed as a cinema on 8th October 1960. Prior to closure it had been specialising in Westerns and a scarcity of this type of film had hastened its demise. The last film shown was *Blackbeard the Pirate* starring William Bendix and Linda Darnell.

The building was subsequently converted over to a Bingo Hall and later demolished to make way for Beamish Court, residential flats.

Projectionists at Albert Hall – George Roberts (left) and Jack Reynoldson.

Below: Albert Hall, 1954.

The Pavilion Cinema, 1954. Opened on 23rd April 1923, it had seating for over 1000 people. The first picture was *Your Best Friend*. The organ was removed in January 1955 to accommodate a wide screen.

The Pavilion Orchestra. Apart from films, the cinema was used for entertainment and occasionally boxing.

Boves of South Moor

Above left: The Bove Family: Raphael, wife Louise and children Albert and Dominic outside their South Moor Shop, *circa* 1944. Raphael left Italy twice to go to America but returned to Scarborough where he worked for Citrone, a relative. He then moved to Spennymoor where he worked as a coal miner. He met his wife Louise who worked for a time at Citrone's at Chester-le-Street. Ralph then moved to Langley Moor where he had a shop and house where Albert was born. Dominic was born in Italy in 1924, staying there a few years due to his mother's ill health. Raphael then bought the South Moor shop from Citrone in 1928. Albert married a Belgian girl while in the army. Dominic took over the shop in 1958. Dominic and Elsie (née Reay) married in 1947. They came out of the shop in 1983 but still have the ice cream factory and vans. Their sons, Michael and Paul, now run the business and the name Bove should be around for many years to come.

Above right: Louise Bove with son Albert. The shop sign shows, L. Bove, Temperance Bar.

Mrs Belle Mould in the doorway of her newsagents shop at 235 Park Road, *circa* 1940. The shop was situated next to Boves. Mrs Mould was one of four generations of her family who have traded as newsagents in South Moor. The business was first started in what is now 256 Park Road in 1898 by William Davison, a former coal miner who worked at Castle Eden and Waterhouses. Mr

Davison had interests in local politics, and was also a Methodist Preacher for nearly 60 years. He was chairman of the Stanley Federation of Newsagents from its inception in 1917. He died, aged 78, of injuries sustained after a fall in the snow while delivering newspapers. He had a wife and four children. The youngest, Belle, was born in South Moor in 1898.

In 1923, Belle married Frederick Mould, a local coal miner and in 1936, on the death of her father, Fred and Belle took over the shop. By 1939 they had moved premises to 235 Park Road. Fred was called into the services during the war and Belle looked after the shop. By 1952, they had again moved premises to 228 Park Road. Their daughter Margaret married Norman Hamflett and when Mr Mould died in 1961, they in turn took over the business. Belle Mould

228 Park Road.

died in 1974 and Norman and Margaret continued running the business together until 1987 when Norman had to retire through ill health.

Daughter, Anne, joined Margaret in the business which by 1999 has been serving and delivering newspapers to the people of South Moor for over 100 years, and is still going. Apart from the business, Margaret, like her grandfather, is still highly involved in the Methodist Church.

Stanley RAFA Branch Club

This branch was formed in 1948 with meetings held in the Imperial Hotel and then at Pinkhams Glove Factory at South Moor. Some of the founder members were: Sid Shimeld, Ralph Daglish, John Wilson, Ron & Norma Firstbrook, Cyril Maddison, June Hopkirk, Alan Aitchieson, Ted Watson, Jim Knott, John Linford and many others.

In 1951, with 36 members, they purchased the Old Wooden Club which was formerly the Central Club in Blooms Avenue, opposite the Albert Hall. It cost £1,000 to buy and adapt into the RAFA Headquarters. At first the members ran the bar until the first steward, George Moffitt was appointed. New premises on the same site were built, and opened by Vice Marshall Bromet on 22nd April 1961.

The Old Wooden Club.

During the 1990s the club has been totally refurbished and they held their 50th anniversary at the end of 1998. The present steward is Terry Conlin. A few names of note in their history are: Ted Longstaff, Bob Reay, Jack Stevens, Sam Parker, Vic Cameron, Cairns Brown DFC and Croix de Guerre, Jack Marshall, Billy Donnelly, Ken Richardson, Bob Rix, Marshall Dodds, Eric Hobbs, Ossie Barrass, Ralph McNeil, Les Nicholl, Tom College, Bill Hodgson, David Underwood, Trevor Paine, and many more names not known at the time of writing.

The interior of the new club, 1961.

The interior of the Old Wooden Club.

Official and committee, February 1960. Back row, left to right: Mr. J. Brady, Mr
N. Kelly, Mr S. Parker, Mr K. Richardson, Mr R. Moscardini, Mr J. Stephenson.
Front row: Mr R. Firstbrook (Welfare Officer), Mr C. Maddison (Chairman),
Miss J. Hobkirk (Club Treasurer), Mr R. Dalglish (President), Mr J. Wilson
(Vice-President), Mr J. Stephens (Secretary).

Eric Lee, Kip Hill Garage, 1946-76.

Eric was born in West Lodge, Beamish Park in 1920. He attended Shield Row School and on leaving, he began working for McCardle at the garage just off Stanley High Street, next to the Gas Works (later Hammells). At 16, he moved to Vickers Armstrong and was employed in general engineering and remained there until the Second World War when he was called into the RAF.

After the war, he left the services as a qualified engineer. In 1946, he decided to build a petrol filling station and garage on land at Kip Hill he had purchased from the Shafto Estates. This land had previously been occupied by Joe Hindhaugh who had kept a dairy herd in byres on the area of land next to the railway.

In addition to the petrol station, Eric also carried out agricultural and automobile engineering and repairs. In 1949, he married Nancy (née Findlaw) at Beamish and they have one daughter, Helen, who is a school teacher. In 1950, Eric Lee was appointed as retail dealer for the Rootes Group (Humber/Hillman) and in the following years sold many new and used cars.

With the new Traffic Act of 1956, Kip Hill Garage became the Ministry of Transport Testing Station for the area. Apart from testing cars and vans, he also for a time road tested Northern General Transport double decker and private hire coaches. The Rootes Group were bought out by Chrysler UK and Eric became part of that organisation. At 5 pm on 31st December 1976, Eric retired after having sold the business to the Fulton Group. The staff at the garage were retained by the new owners at Eric's request.

Since retirement, Eric has kept up most of his many interests such as the Methodist Church, a Director of the Stanley Building Society, a Trustee of the Methold Alms Houses of the Beamish Estates, a former President of the Stanley Rotary Club, a Friend of Beamish, walking and watching football and cricket. Eric and his wife Nancy still live in Beamish Park where he is still an active member of the community.

Right: J.R. Watson, Fairview Garage, Beamish Street. Right to left: J.R. Watson, son Ernest and trainee, Billy Thirlwell, *circa* 1935. Mr Watson was the son of a travelling draper from Bedlington. His father travelled

the area with his horse and cart taking drapery orders. He wanted his son to follow him into the trade but John wanted to be a saddler and he was apprenticed to Teasdale in Dipton. He met Mary Anne Harland at Annfield Plain and they married at View Lane Church. For some time they lived at Pontop Pike before he opened his first saddler's shop adjacent to what is now Stanley Council Offices. Later he bought a shop opposite with the flat above (now Shoefayre). He traded there for many years as a saddler, also selling hardware, ironmongery and bicycles. They had three children, Ernest, Sarah Anne (Sadie) and Freda. During the depression, Mr Watson allowed young unemployed men to use his large billiard table in the attic for a few pennies. These pennies were saved up, and once a year, Mr Watson provided tents, transport and food free of charge for these men to go camping. In 1930 he had a house and shop (Fairview) built in Beamish Street. With changing times and needs he decided to diversify and erected a garage and filling station next to the house. The garage was erected from old wooden army huts. The family maintained the shop while he and his son, Ernest, built up the garage business. As a hobby, Mr Watson was an accomplished model maker as shown in the photograph below and he won many competitions. The workmanship was of the finest quality and detail. His wife Mary Ann died in 1940 and he died in 1942. The family kept the business going until 1966 when the shop finally closed. The only surviving daughter, Freda, still resides at Fairview. The garage is now a motor spares shop and the shop is a household electrical appliance shop.

CHURCHES

St Stephen's Church in South Stanley has always had a strong Mothers' Union and this early group taken *circa* 1959 included the following: M. Menear, Mrs Oyston, the Rev and Mrs Butler, B. O'Neil, S. Vittie, R. Rutter, E. Vittie, R. Gilfellon, Mrs Morton, M. Smailes, Mrs Padget, Mrs Parnell, M. McIlvaney, N. Robertson, and J. Hart.

St Stephen's Church, South Stanley

St Stephen's Church, South Stanley opened in 1954. When the Rev Sturges left, there was a farewell service as pictured here with members of the clergy, choir and congregation.

This photograph of a large group at St Stephen's was probably taken at the 10th Anniversary Service in 1964.

St Mary's R.C. Church, Hustledown

In May 1930, Father Dix proposed to the Bishop of Hexham & Newcastle the building of a new church at Hustledown for the people of Bloomfontein, Craghead, South Moor and South Stanley.

Permission for the building of a new church was given on 9th February 1931. The Towneley family donated the land at Hustledown. There was little progress until January 1932 when architects Kitching of Darlington submitted plans which were passed in February. The church was to be similar in many ways to the one at Saltburn. In March 1932, Mr Kindred of Sunniside submitted a tender for £2,761 for the building of the church (excluding the oak work).

Building commenced on 13th April 1932 under the supervision of Father Dix. The Foundation Stone was laid by Dr Joseph Thormon, Bishop of Newcastle on 28th May 1932 after a procession from the nearby Catholic School. The estimated cost of the church was £4,000 and it was named St Mary's. The Dedication Service by Bishop Thormon took place on 16th November 1932 with over 60 priests in attendance plus a huge congregation. After the dedication, the first High Pontifical Mass was

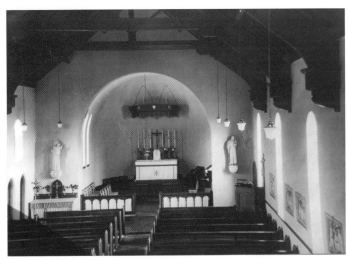

View of Altar from balcony.

held in the new church.

On the 20th November 1932 some 600 people attended Mass at St Mary's. The Stations of the Cross donated by 14 parishioners were erected by Father Pickering at an Evening Service on 2nd December 1932. Hundreds of people attended the First Midnight Mass Service in the church on Christmas Eve 1932.

Silver Jubilee of the Church.

Clergy who have served the Parish

Father Pickering was in the care of the Parish from 1922 and lived in the School House. He was appointed Parish Priest on 10th August 1934. Sadly he was killed in a road accident on 4th April 1946.

Father Scriven was appointed Parish Priest on 6th April 1946. He died at South Moor on 9th November 1973.

Curates who served under Father Scriven:

Father K. Mulcahy 1956-59
Father F. Robinson 1959-66
Father J. Doherty 1966-69
Father M. McKenna 1969-74.

Father W. McKenna was appointed Parish Priest in September 1974. He retired on health grounds in July 1984.

Father J. Park was appointed Parish Priest in September 1984 and served for two years. He is now Parish Priest of St Joseph's, Stanley.

Father Scriven.

Father J.T. Connelly was appointed Parish Priest in September 1986, retired in June 1991. He died at his home 2nd April 1992.

Father T. Dollard was appointed Parish Priest in June 1991. He died while playing golf in September 1992.

Father D. Tindale was appointed Parish Priest in December 1992.

Left to right: Fathers Leo and Wilfred Pickering and seated Father Dix.

Births, Marriages & Deaths

First Baptism – Winnifred Morrison, 18th November 1932.

First Wedding – J.F. McAninley to W.V. Shields, 8th September 1934.

Earliest Funeral – P. Banon, 1st November 1934.

Stanley Salvation Army Band, 1932. Stanley had a fine history of producing some excellent musicians in the Army Band. Included in the photograph is Billy Blackett who was Boys' World Champion Trombone Player.

Park Road Methodist Church Sunday School. The Primary Department of the Sunday School is pictured in the church at the time of the 50th Anniversary in 1948.

The Bells of St Andrew's

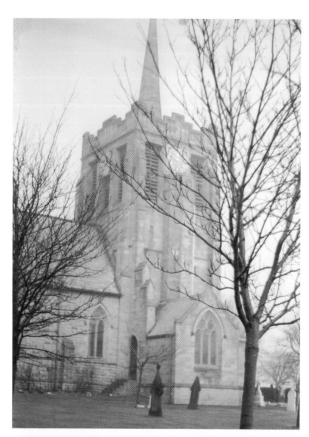

St Andrew's Church was extended in 1930 and at that time the bells were installed with separate donations of £1,000 each by Lord Joicey and Mrs Charlton of Wylam in memory of their sons who were killed in the First World War. At the time when the bells were first rang, hundreds of local people came out of their houses to hear them.

Below: Pictured in the belfry next to the bells are Alan Gibson (right) and Cyril Wright. Access to the tower is by way of a spiral staircase.

Alan Gibson is shown in 1997 playing the bells. Some of the known bell ringers over the years include: Tom Harrison, Norma Firstbrook, Cissie Haste, Uren Ross, Marjorie Baldwin, Tot Hindhaugh, Mattie Purvis, Jean Reed, Gordon Chapman, Alan Gibson and Inez Watson.

The Rev John Crennell

The Rev John Crennell was instrumental in the formation of Beamish Parish side by side with his senior, the Rev John Mathwin, the Vicar of Tanfield. In 1873, John Crennell took charge of the rapidly increasing mining district of West Stanley. Services were conducted in Stanley National School which had been licensed for Divine Worship since 21st January 1868.

John set himself the task of raising the funds to build a church at Stanley and St Andrew's was consecrated in 1876. Apart from St Andrew's, Rev Crennell was also responsible for the building of St Andrew's Vicarage, St Andrew's Institute, St Columba's Mission Church at Oxhill, and St Cuthbert's Mission Church at East Stanley.

Rev John Crennell
VICAR OF BEAMISH
1876   1895

He was a very outspoken cleric and very close to the working man, often offending the local gentry by speaking in defence of the downtrodden working class. After one such sermon, he concluded:

'I would rather that my grave should be watered by the tears of widows and orphans, and others I have tried to help, than have erected to my memory, the finest marble monument man could design.'

The Rev Crennell was made Rector of Byers Green in 1895 and died while staying with his friend, the Rev Moscrop on 11th September 1897.

Annfield Plain Wesleyan Methodist Church (St John's)

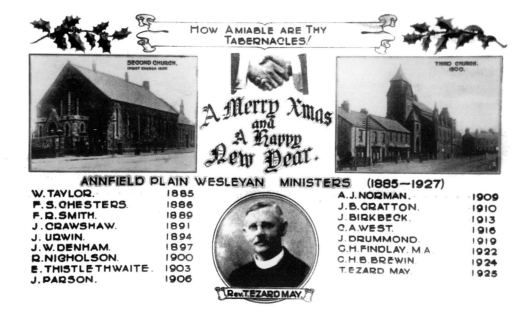

HOW AMIABLE ARE THY TABERNACLES!

SECOND CHURCH. (FIRST CHURCH 1854)

THIRD CHURCH. 1900.

A Merry Xmas and A Happy New Year.

ANNFIELD PLAIN WESLEYAN MINISTERS (1885—1927)

Minister	Year	Minister	Year
W. TAYLOR.	1885	A. J. NORMAN.	1909
F. S. CHESTERS.	1886	J. B. GRATTON.	1910
F. R. SMITH.	1889	J. BIRKBECK.	1913
J. CRAWSHAW.	1891	C. A. WEST.	1916
J. URWIN.	1894	J. DRUMMOND.	1919
J. W. DENHAM.	1897	G. H. FINDLAY. M.A.	1922
R. NICHOLSON.	1900	C. H. B. BREWIN.	1924
E. THISTLETHWAITE.	1903	T. EZARD MAY.	1925
J. PARSON.	1906		

Rev. T. EZARD MAY.

This Christmas Postcard is a little misleading as records show there were probably four churches.

Prior to 1850, the Wesleyans in the Annfield Plain area held services at various locations – Nellie Forster's cottage, Priscilla Bell's cottage, John Lawson's house, Mackie's Schoolroom in West Road, and a cottage near Mrs Reed's shop.

They decided to build a church near Pontop Rows and this brick built church opened on 9th May 1854. The church was later rebuilt and enlarged but coal workings caused the church to subside and it was taken down. Messrs Joicey & Co paid £400 damages. A third church was built on this site costing £720 and opened in 1870.

From 1861-1881, the local population trebled from 3,718 to 10,147 so a schoolroom was added and opened in 1887.

By 1896 and due to overcrowding, it was decided to build a new large amphitheatre type church and extra land was secured in 1899. The new church opened in June 1890 and was known as the Wesleyan Church. The cost of building this church was cleared by 1904. The wooden tower was replaced by a stone battlement in 1929.

Methodist Union took place in 1932 and the church was re-named St John's. This church closed in 1963 when the members joined with Catchgate Methodist Free Church. The Light of the World windows were removed from St John's and installed into the Methodist Free Church. St John's was later demolished.

Dipton Primitive Methodists
A Centenary Account 1823-1923

The Dipton Methodists held their Centenary on 23rd August 1923. During this time, they had three separate churches. The first Camp Meeting was held at Colliery Dykes in June 1823 when George Pierson visited Dipton. As a result of this meeting, classes taken by Mr Humphrey were held in the village. In August 1823, Thomas Batty and Jeremiah Gilbert visited Dipton and it was this visit that the centenary celebrated. They decided to build a chapel at Flint Hill known as 'The Ranters Chapel' in 1834 and this chapel seated 80 people and cost £60. Many of the men who attended this chapel were employed at Dickinson's Pit.

Flint Hill Ranters Chapel.

Left: The second church was built in Dipton opposite the Bute Arms in 1873 costing £920 mainly by the efforts of Ralph Shields. This is now a builders' premises.

Right: The church today. The building of the third church began on 26th May 1906 when a group of men and young boys marched from the old church up to the site of the new church.

This church opened on 23rd February 1907 and cost £3,060. The architects were Davison & Phillipson. Thomas Reynoldson and his son Robert were in charge of building while

Mr Robert Southern was in charge of the joinery. The church was opened by Jane Swallows of Dunston and the Sunday School was opened by Newcastle Councillor, Anthony Oates. Sermons on the opening day were by the Rev E. French and Mr Joseph Longstaff assisted by Circuit Minister Rev B. Dennison and Mr A. Longstaff.

Annfield Plain Central Methodist Church

Right: The church in 1946 at the time of their 50th Jubilee Celebrations.

Below: Sunday School Primary Department, 1946. Leaders: Misses, A. Bainbridge, N. Mordue, I. Chambers and J. Bailes.

Bottom: Sunday School Junior Department, 1946. Superintendent J.T. Wilkinson, Secretary A. Murray.

South Stanley Methodist Chapel congregation on the site of the new chapel at the end of Cleveland Terrace just behind Durham Road in 1959.

Members of Oxhill Church Sunday School with some of the Sunday School Teachers and Leaders in the back street of Joicey Terrace, Oxhill in the 1950s. They would go around the streets singing hymns raising money for church funds. Included in the group are: Miles Armstrong, Maureen Danby, Shirley Armstrong, Norma Jeans, Janet Vincent, Audrey Snailham, members of the Oyston family, Edward Carrington, Vera Chapman, Albert Fawcett, Margaret Foreman, Marion Diss, Delcia Diss, J. Tuckerman, Adam Wilkinson, S. Woods. ? Woods, N. Hall, B. McVitie and G. Sharp playing the organ (extreme right). Sunday School was popular with local children and the highlight of every year was the 'Sunday School Anniversary'.

Craghead Primitive Church 60th Anniversary 1890-1950.

The church in 1950. This is now converted into a splendid house occupied by Mr and Mrs Craggs and family.

Sunday School Senior and Junior Girls, 1950. The Sunday School opened 22nd September 1891.

Craghead PM Church Sunday School Senior and Junior Boys, 1950. This church amalgamated with Craghead Wesleyans in 1962.

Tantobie Wesleyan Methodist Church. This was one of the first Methodist Churches in this area and it opened in 1892. It was a grand structure with the church on the upper level and Sunday School and Meeting Rooms below. The Wesleyans and the Primitive Methodists amalgamated with the services being held in the White-le-Head Primitive Methodist Church. For several years the old church was used as a television sales and repair workshop.

Greencroft Methodist Church

Greencroft Methodists had three churches. In 1870 there were approximately 50 houses in Greencroft Village and a chapel was formed in a downstairs room at 4 Long Brick Rows. This room had a small pulpit, a wooden choir pew and wooden forms for the congregation.

In 1888, money was borrowed interest free from Mr Phillip Reay to build a new church. Church members – Bell, Manners, Wilkinson, Rennison and others dug out the foundations. The stones were quarried by J. Elliott and D. Plews, the builders were Mr Johnson (brickwork) and Mr Mordue (woodwork). The Foundation Stone was laid in 1888 and the church opened the following year in Old Greencroft. Their first Sunday School trip was to Shotley Bridge in coal carts loaned by Pontop Colliery.

In 1902, the chapels were badly affected by pitfalls and 50 loads of ballast were tipped into the hole created by one such pitfall. In 1910, Mr Ritson donated the site for a new church (pictured below) but little progress was made until 1928 when the old chapel was sold. Architect Richardson of Stockton submitted plans in 1929 and the chosen contractor was Rendle with a tender of £2,685. The Stone Laying Ceremony took place in April 1930 and the church officially opened in November 1930. In 1943 the Boys Brigade was formed and also in 1943, the debt of the church was cleared and the deeds handed over on 13th May.

This church was known as 'The Singing Church' due to its excellent choir. In 1946, they were granted a licence to solemnise marriages and the first wedding was between Mary Dixon and Ronald Jewel.

By 1967, the membership had dropped dramatically and they also discovered dry rot in the building. The estimates for repair were very high so at a meeting, it was decided to close the church, but this did not happen at once.

At the Christmas Service, Mr Phillip Robinson was requested to sing 'The Holy City' amidst great emotion. The last baptism in the church was that of Lesley Armin.

The church finally closed on 24th August 1968, when the site was gifted to Annfield Plain Central Methodists and the balance of £1,054 was shared between the Manchester Church Investment Fund (£800) and £80 each to Annfield Plain Central Methodists, Catchgate Methodists and the Methodist Circuit.

COLLIERIES

The Morrison Busty Colliery Band in 1926. The local MP, Jimmy Glanville, is shown standing at the extreme right. He was himself a former miner and represented the Consett Constituency of which Stanley was a part for many years.

The Collieries of Craghead

Craghead Colliery, circa 1940.

William Hedley came to Craghead in January 1839 and began to sink the William Pit to the Hutton Seam. He also constructed a self acting incline railway line to take the coals down to join the Stanhope & Tyne Railway. Hedley died in 1843 and the business was carried on by his four sons, Thomas, William, George and Oswald. The family went on to sink several other shafts, including:

The George in 1854; The Oswald in 1878; The Edward in 1909 to the Hutton and in 1919 to the Brockwell.

The Thomas and George had seams to Thomas, Shield Row and Five Quarter.
The Oswald had seams to Mauldlin, Low Main and Hutton.
The Busty had seams to Towneley top and bottom, Busty and Brockwell.

The depth of the seams ranged from 41 fathoms to 163 fathoms. The narrowest seams were 2 feet at the Oswald and Busty, and the thickest was 5 feet at the Thomas and George. There was a seam of 18 inches in the Victoria Seam at 170 fathoms but this was never worked.

As the coalfield developed, housing was needed for the miners and their families, and the first colliery houses in the village were built in short terraces at Wagtail Cottages. These primitive style cottages were built by Walton & Marshall, costing £45 to build. They consisted of two rooms, one up and one down with only one door.

While sinking the William Pit, good quality clay was found below the Five Quarter Seam so the Hedleys opened a brickworks in Craghead next to the William Pit. Other streets of houses followed, such as Thomas Street, William Street and Edward Street. The brickworks closed after better clay was found at South Moor. When it was realised there were large deposits of coal in the area, the coal owners decided to

The Oswald Pit.

build bigger and better houses to keep their workforce in the village.

Coal mining production in Craghead ceased in 1968. It seemed for a while the village would die, but the people have stayed and Craghead has lasted long after the coal has gone.

The Edward & Busty Pits.

A group of officials at the Craghead Busty Pit Shaft and Winder.

Coal miners John Soulsby and Gordon Liddle with pit pony 'Fox' in the Craghead Busty Pit Stables. This colliery eventually closed on 11th April 1969. Some miners transferred to other collieries while others were made redundant.

'The Fortune Pit Yard' by Jim Bradley. This watercolour is one of a set of four of Burnhope Colliery painted by accomplished local artist Jim Bradley in 1986. Jim is the son of a former Burnhope coal miner, John Bradley. The view is of the Fortune Pit Yard, East Wood Row, Snaiths House, Church and Church Row.

Jim Bradley was born in 1948 and lived at South View, Burnhope, for twenty-two years. He studied Art and Industrial Design for four years at Newcastle College of Art before training as a teacher. His first teaching post as an art teacher was at Heaton School, Newcastle for two years before moving to St Mary's Sixth Form College at Middlesbrough, teaching Art, Design and Technology. Jim is presently Director of Studies (senior teacher) at Stanley School of Technology and still teaches Art. He now lives at Lanchester and spends most of his spare time painting water colours of local scenes. His latest commissioned painting is for Alec Stewart, the England cricket captain.

The Annie Pit, Burnhope. Empty wagons stand at the back of the Annie and Fortune Pits.

The Annie Pit Winding Engine. The engine was installed in 1868. It was a single cylinder, horizontal drop valve engine fitted with Stephenson reversing gear, built by G. Joicey & Co of Newcastle. It had a 5' 9" stroke x 36 " bore.

These men at the Annie Pit are at the bottom of the steps which lead up to the winder. Included are: Bunty Smith (banksman), Jack Souter (winding engineman), Mick Curry (shaftsman), Andrew Scott (winding engineman), J. Thompson (who supplied this photograph) worked with the two enginemen until the pit closed in 1949.

Burnhope Colliery

The Burnhope Banner at Durham.

Tanfield Lea Colliery

This is an early photograph of Tanfield Lea Colliery, note the tall chimney. Joicey first took over the colliery in 1842 and for many years life centred around the pit, with housing, school and churches built. Much of the old housing is long gone, replaced by fine modern homes.

All local colliery Miners' Lodges had their own Pit Banner usually made of silk and decorated to the highest standard. The banners had several functions; for example: to lead the parade at times of tragedy, disaster, miners meetings and celebrations. It was a great honour to carry the banner into such places as the Miners' Gala at Durham. The Tanfield Lea Banner is shown with the following: Front row: G. Armstrong, J. Fisher, T. Robson, C. Bartell, J. Stephens, C. Brannen. Back Row: W. Pratt, A. Grundy, T. Rockett, T. Watkins and W. Holden. The names of the two men on the poles are not known. Tanfield Lea Colliery closed in August 1962.

Tanfield Lea Colliery Pit Baths. These baths were opened in 1958. They were a great asset both to the miners and their wives. For many years, they had to put up with the old tin bath in front of the fire before bathrooms were installed in their houses. It was a big change for the coal miner to be able to go home clean and to leave his work clothes at the pit.

Tanfield Lea North Pit, 1960.

The Hedley Pit Heroes

On the 29th September 1930, a roof fall occurred in the Hedley Pit, South Moor. A coal hewer named Frederick Beaumount was partially buried in the fall. Chargeman, Victor King was the first to come to the rescue. He found that a small passageway remained open by which the buried miner might be reached. King was assisted by his son Richard and fellow miner, John George Tarn. They immediately built two chocks of timber to keep the way open. The

The Hedley Pit.

passageway was approximately seven yards long and two feet square and the only practical method of rescue was for three men to crawl along the passageway and lie full length, two in the passageway, and one over the body of Beaumont to protect him from falling stones, which were passed back one at a time. This perilous and arduous task carried on for nine hours by a team of workers, working in relays under the directions of the manager, Mr Walter Robert Scott, and under manager Robert Reed, until at last Beaumont was freed, shaken but otherwise unhurt. During the whole nine hours the roof was 'shifting' and 'trickling', and on four occasions, Beaumont was almost freed when a further fall buried him again. At one time, the danger of a further fall was so great that the manager phoned for Dr Fox to come to the Pit so as to amputate Beaumont's leg and so expedite his release. Fortunately as it turned out, there was insufficient arm room for the doctor to carry out the amputation, but the doctor remained on the scene until Beaumont was rescued, and he examined and treated him before sending him to the surface. Shortly after Beaumont was extricated, the tunnel collapsed. There were 19 men in all involved with the rescue. On 30th December 1931, the 19 rescuers received the Carnegie Award for bravery in recognition of their brave endeavour. The presentation was at West Stanley. On 26th February 1932, at an Investiture at Buckingham Palace, the 19 men were awarded the Edward Medal by King George V for their outstanding bravery. The 19 men were: Jack Akers, Thomas Buckley, Philip Cox, John Dart, T. Dixon, Dr C.J.B. Fox, Bob Johnson, Victor King, Richard King, Joseph Kent, Joseph Lees, George Mason, George Nancollas, Robert Reed, Walter Scott, Walter Sheldrake, John G. Tarn, Thomas Uren and William Waugh.

The Hedley Pit Heroes.

Stanley Pit Rescue Team training at Houghton-le-Spring. Joseph Hall is second from the right.

Louisa New Pit Rescue Team, 1912.

The Burnhope Colliery Band in the 1920s. Burnhope, like most pit villages had its own colliery band. The members were mostly employed in the local colliery and Burnhope's band is pictured with the pit banner in the village. Included are: Joe Moss, Joe Briggs, Tot Robson, John Bradley, Tommy Chapman and ? Chatton.

The Burnhope Banner shown going to the Miners' Gala.

The shaft bottom at the Fortune Pit, Burnhope. This colliery was unusual to
our area as the boiler was underground. The five men shown at the shaft
bottom are: Jack Thompson, Tommy Walters, John Bradley, Ken Lumley and
Andrew Heslop.

Bank Hands at Burnhope Colliery: George Jackson, Billy Wilson, E. Bailey,
W. Bennet, Isaac Rushton, Jack Souter, Bunty Smith, Matt Gray, Tommy
Laverick and J.R. Smith jnr.

Miners' Sundays

The local miners joined together to hold a service, sometimes at Murray Park, and on this occasion at the Kings Head Field. The parade is shown passing the bottom of Stanley Street.

The bands, local clergy, speakers and the miners and their families at the service on the Kings Head Field.

The Delight Pit, Dipton

The Delight Pit opened in 1842. This view of the pit yard shows the stock pile of timber, much used in coal mining as supports, coal wagons, and the winding gear and workshops.

Dipton Colliery, sadly shown standing derelict after closure. Like many other local villages, Dipton thrived for many years on coal mining, but now we have no collieries left, only the memories.

Beamish Mary Colliery

Beamish Mary Colliery opened in 1883/4 and closed in April 1966.

A Beamish Miner – This miner is typical of many miners before the time of the pit baths. He would travel as he was from the pit and get out of his pit clothes before bathing in the kitchen. It was usually the wife's job to scrub the miner's back and she also had the task of dadding the pit clothes once they had dried.

Beamish Mary Colliery
Vertical Winding Engine.

Bill Nicholson at the controls
of the old steam winding
engine at Beamish Mary
Colliery in 1948. Chris
Armstrong was also winder
man at Beamish.

The Dipton Colliery Pit Ponies, Busty Seam, June 1921.

The Burns Pit Disaster

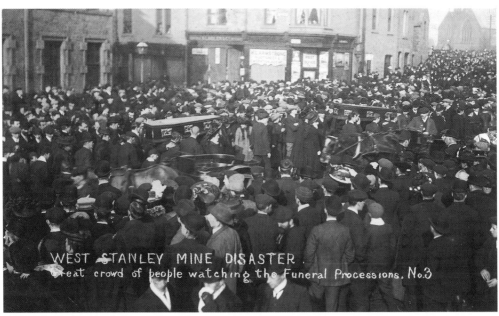

WEST STANLEY MINE DISASTER.
Great crowd of people watching the Funeral Processions. No.3

This disaster was the worst ever in our local history when 168 men and boys tragically lost their lives in the quest for coal. The disaster happened on Tuesday, 16th February 1909. The scene in this photograph is of the great struggle through the crowds for the relatives to get their loved ones to the church for burial in the mass graves at St Andrew's.

The Locomotives of Craghead Colliery

The Burnhopeside, driven by W.G. Robson.

Wm Hedley jnr introduced locomotives to Craghead Collieries with the *Wylam Dilly* in 1862 where it remained until 1879.

The second engine came in 1879 and was built by the Dunston Engineering Works at Gateshead.

Burnhopeside was probably a prototype engine made by Black Hawthorne for the 1887 Newcastle Exhibition and named *Victoria* by the manufactures. It was bought by Wm Hedley jnr in 1887 but before he took delivery, he insisted the name be changed to 'Burnhopeside' after the residence of Hedley. The engine's early colours were light and dark green, lined with black and red. In 1947, when the mines were nationalised, the colours were changed to NCB blue and the engine re-numbered to 38. This locomotive was scrapped in 1957.

Holmside No. 2 was an engine built in 1901 by Chapman Ferneaux & Co and worked between Craghead Pit and the Morrison Busty. After nationalisation, this engine was re-numbered 35. It was scrapped in 1962.

Holmside Engines Nos 3 &4 were saddle tank engines built by Hawthorne Leslie (date unknown). After nationalisation they were re-numbered 36 and 37. No 3 was garaged at Craghead engine shed and remained at the colliery until the closure of the pit.

NCB Locomotive No 80 was a locomotive built by Robert Stephenson & Hawthorn and came to Craghead in 1949 and worked at the colliery until 1967 when it was transferred to Handon Hold engine sheds along with Engine No 36. The transportation of coal by road was virtually the end at Craghead for the locomotives.

Byermoor Colliery

This selection of photographs of Byermoor Colliery was taken in 1963. Although Byermoor is outside the boundary line, many Stanley miners worked both there and Marley Hill.

The Upcast Shaft.

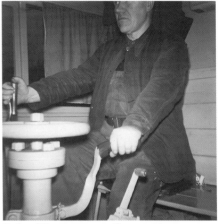

John Thompson, the engine winderman (born at Burnhope).

A group of surface workers: Ronnie Richardson (safety officer), Fred Watson and Bob Gray (both joiners), Jackie Nelson (blacksmith) and George Elliott (blacksmith) up the ladder.

SPORT

'The Usual Suspects' – a line up of boxing talent at Stanley Boys' Club in the early 1950s. Left to right: Ray Chesterfield, Leo Hodgson, Terry O'Hanlon, Charlie Gregg, Tom Gibb, G. O'Neill. The club opened on 1st November 1937 and was requisitioned by the Armed Forces during the Second World War. The club was visited by the Duke of Gloucester in November 1954.

West Stanley Amateur Football Club (AFC) and Murray Park

The club was founded as Oakeys Lilywhites in 1889 and matches were played at Oakeys Oval, which had an enclosure and a grandstand. Friendly matches eventually led to a season in the Northwest Durham Alliance League in 1895. They subsequently joined the Northern Alliance League in 1896 and immediately had a name change imposed upon them when Oakeys Lilywhites became Stanley FC. Their last game under the old name took place at the Oval on 29th August 1896 when they beat Birtley 3-1. Stanley FC's first game under the new title took place on 12th September 1896 with a 0-1 away defeat at Jarrow.

Stanley were now playing in the company of such clubs as Ashington, Newcastle United reserves and Sunderland 'A' team. In the 1905-06 season they were placed 3rd in a table of 16 teams (16 games won and 4 drawn) finishing only 4 points behind the champions Willington. Their last game at the old Oval enclosure took place on 30th April 1906, a friendly game against Hull City which the local team won 5-3.

Plans had been made and construction was well underway for a new stadium. Before completion Stanley's application for entry into the newly formed North Eastern League was accepted.

The completion of the Murray Park ground was accomplished just one hour before kick off for the first game of the new season, a Durham Challenge Cup match on Thursday 27th September 1906 against Stanley United FC from Crook, which ended in a 1-1 draw. The club had a new name West Stanley AFC and the first home league game produced a goal less draw against the third team of Middlesbrough. By the season close the club finished in a very satisfactory 3rd position and plans were underway for improvements to the stadium and pitch.

The club had reasonable success during their early seasons in the league but several of their most talented players were lost to Football League clubs. Extra revenue for the club was also provided through the occasional good FA Cup run.

A party of players and officials outside the Houses of Parliament prior to the club's momentous game at White Hart Lane. Aneurin Williams (MP for Consett) stands in the middle of the picture (hat in right hand).

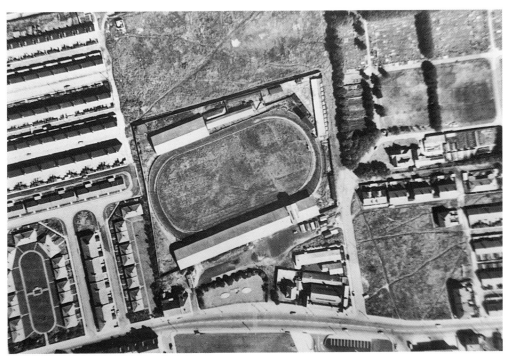

Aerial view of the stadium in 1966.

Following the First World War the club embarked on perhaps their most momentous season. Despite a disappointing low mid-table place in the league the club's FA Cup exploits would become legendary. The West Stanley team would eventually progress to the 2nd round proper and joined the last 32 clubs of the competition.

In the 6th qualifying round on 20th December 1919 the local team entertained Rotherham County of the Football League 2nd Division, roared on by over 8,000 fans, they triumphed 2-0. Gillingham from the Southern League were Stanley's visitors in the 1st round proper and were seen off 3-1 before a crowd estimated at over 10,000.

Tottenham Hotspur F.C. topping the 2nd Division and FA Cup winners 19 years earlier as a non-league team entertained Stanley for the 2nd round. A crowd of 35,000 paid £2,500 entrance fees to see the London team triumph 4-0 and bring the gallant run of the non-leaguers to an end.

An application was made in the 1920-21 season to join the proposed Football League Division 3 (North) but a moderate season did not assist them in the poll for places, receiving only 6 votes, far too few for acceptance.

On the 27th October 1921 a second replay of the final of the NW Durham Challenge Cup against Leadgate Park, saw the club's all-time record attendance at Murray Park of 12,585. Fans paid £472 to see West Stanley fail by a single goal.

With the depression of the 1920s attendances at all grounds began to fall though Stanley were still fairly well supported compared to some older teams in the league. The early '30s continued in much the same vein and by the start of 1936 the club was in dire straits.

A lifeline was thrown when an organisation allied to greyhound racing offered to become tenants of Murray Park. The 1936-37 season ended with West Stanley finishing 10 points below the next club having had only 2 wins,

3 draws, and 33 defeats, which left little alternative, but to accept the situation or disband.

In late August 1937 the first greyhound meeting took place before a crowd of some 5,000 people in the renamed 'The Stanley Greyhound Racing Stadium'. It was necessary to reduce the length of the football pitch in order to accommodate the dog track oval, which made it smaller than the minimum requirements for FA Cup games, an important bearing on the club's eventual demise.

Following the Second World War, a renewed interest was taken in football and in 1950 North Shields were crowned champions for the first time with West Stanley only 2 points behind. However, attendances began declining again and with FA Cup matches now denied them the club was finding it increasingly difficult to retain their best players.

The 1957-58 season was the last for all the Football League reserve teams in the league, which lead eventually to the end of the competition. West Stanley were forced to enter the Northern Alliance for what would prove to be their last season – 1958-59. The last match for the club was on 25th April 1959, a 1-1 home draw with Alnwick Town.

On 13th August the announcement was made that the club and team could not carry on. Whilst lack of finance was the primary problem the occasional clashing of fixtures with the greyhounds, the undersize pitch and subsidence due to colliery workings all compounded the situation. Clearly the ground and pitch were no longer suitable for senior football.

Hopes were entertained in the early 1960s of reforming the team and club with a view to playing in the nearby King's Head playing field, but only £600 was raised towards the £4,000 cost of fencing etc. and the scheme fell through.

The ground itself continued with greyhound racing, being partially rebuilt following a fire in 1971, and yet another fire in the late 1980s when the Huntingdon night club, which had risen on the site of the 1971 fire, was itself engulfed in flames. Meetings became more difficult to put together and attendances declined accordingly. Finally in 1994 the stadium closed forever and over three quarters of a century's sporting activities in the ground ceased.

A subsequent fire, destroying the TOTE board and demolition of the existing buildings has lain the area to waste. The outer perimeter wall still stands but the old area stands forlorn, its dog track and inner field overgrown with grass and weeds.

A recent view of Murray Park – derelict after demolition

Fred Stansfield

Fred was another great all round sportsman and athlete. He was well known at football, cricket, athletics and tennis and a great competitor at whatever he did.

Fred Stansfield

He played first for Annfield Plain County School under 11s football team. In 1949, the team won the League and Shimelds Cup. He then went to Annfield Plain Secondary Modern where as a first year he went straight into the football team. While there, he also played for three seasons for Stanley & District and for Durham County Schools for two seasons. He was also chosen to play in an International Trial game when he played alongside Bobby Charlton.

League clubs Burnley, Newcastle United and Sunderland approached him and at 15 he signed for Sunderland in 1953, and was soon playing for the A team. By the age of 16, he was playing for the Reserves in the North Eastern League. At 17, Fred signed professional for Sunderland and played in the Northern Intermediate League. He played outside right in a first team trial game with Len Shackleton inside right and Stan Anderson at right half. Sunderland manager Bill Murray retired and new manager Alan Brown put Fred on the transfer list and he moved to Gateshead in 1957. He then played Non-League football for Consett, Annfield Plain, Spennymoor, York City, Craghead and Sherburn Hill. Apart from the odd injury Fred played every Saturday for 16 years.

At athletics he won Victor Ludorum at Annfield Pain Secondary School at both Junior and Senior levels and also ran for the District and in County trials. At tennis he played for Annfield Plain Tennis Club and in 1961-63, he and partner Ray Pallister never lost a match in two seasons. At cricket, Fred played for Annfield Plain Juniors and Second team and also played for Ransome Hoffman & Pollard.

Annfield Plain AFC, 1961-62. Back row, left to right: Gordon Taylor, Dick Stansfield, Eddie Eccleston, Wilf Hobson, Tommy Carrick, Hughy Murphy. Front row: Marshal Lawson, Fred Stansfield, Harry Randall, Lenny Scott and Hugh Boyle.

Albert Steward

Albert is shown being carried shoulder high with the FA Amateur Cup at Wembley in 1959 when he captained Crook Town to victory. This was a great honour for a local lad. He was the winner of two FA Amateur Cup winners' medals with Crook Town. The first of these was against Bishop Auckland in 1954 when it took three games to decide the winners. The first game at Wembley on 10th April 1954 ended 2-2 in front of 100,000 supporters. The second game was played at Newcastle on 19th April and ended 2-2 in front of a crowd of 60,000. The third, and deciding game, was played at Middlesbrough on 22nd April 1954 in front of 40,000 supporters when Crook eventually won 1-0. This was then a record in both overall attendance of over 200,000 and gate money, even beating the professional Cup competition. Tommy Riley of Tanfield Lea also played in the 1954 Final.

The second winners' medal was against Barnet at Wembley on 8th April 1959 when Crook won 3-2. The 1959 team are shown (not in order): Ray Snowball, Derek Gardener, Bert Steward (captain), Derek Carr, Colin Bainbridge, Ray Wilkie, Arnold Coates, Seamus O'Connell, Brian Keating, Mike Tracey and Jimmy McMillan.

Albert had at that time been playing for Crook since 1952. He was also a very good cricketer and played for South Moor before moving to Consett in the Tyneside Senior League. He lived at Annfield Plain and was a chemist at Consett Steel Works. In 1999, Albert still lives at Greencroft with his wife Joyce.

South Moor Greenland Junior School, League champions, League Cup winners, RAFA Cup winners, 1965-66. Photographed with Mr A.C. Gurkin (left) and Head Teacher Mr O. Barrass are back row, left to right: R. Smith, R. Wanless, J. Howden, A. Johnson, R. Robinson, J. Hilland, K. Johnson. Front row: D. Robinson, P. Carleton, W. Carr, S. Hind, L. Hutchinson, I. Young.

Craghead Junior School football team, winners of the League and Shimeld Cup, 1959-60. Photographed with Mr O. Barrass are back row, left to right: M. Oughton, W. Lewins, T. Scott, K. Bell, J. Ord, K. Murphy, A. Scott, A. Foggan, J. White. Front row: H. Morton, K. Rutherford, E. Tempest, A. Corbett, W. Coulson.

Annfield Plain Junior School football team, 1948-49. The team of 1948-49 season was very successful and won both the League and Cup competitions. The team are pictured with their families and members of staff in the school yard. The team were left to right: Dennis Talbot, Edgar Wilson, John Densham, Fred Stansfield, Harry Statt, Edwin Dalkin, Billy Fawcett, Alan Miles, Tommy Henderson, John Stevens and Alan Westwater. Not shown in photograph is Alan Jackson,

Annfield Plain County School football team, 1949. This team of 1949 needed new football strips, so the school used the old wartime blackout curtains for the material. The team and staff are, back row, left to right: Alan Hands, Alan Curry, Harry Secome

(headmaster), Jack Golightly (teacher), Joe Gibbons (teacher), Albert Snowdon, Eric Dodds. Front row: Bobby Nichols, Eddie Price, Joe Mills, Alwin Sowdon, Alister Hunter, Richard Stansfield, John Armstrong.

Craghead Junior School football team, 1962-63. Pictured with teachers Mr
Oswald Johnson (left) and Mr Ossie Barrass are, back row, left to right:
R. Montgomery, unknown, J. Emery, Keith Irvin, J. Coulson, R. Sutton.
D. Armstrong, Peter Riley. Front row: P. Montgomery, A. Cape, P. Comerford,
J. Wilkinson, A. Snailam, ? Wallace.

South Moor Social Club 'Mickey's' football team. Back row, left to right:
W. Coulson, R. Liddell, M. Irwin, G. Bailey, J. Coulson, F. Walker. Front row:
M. Bowerbanks, J. Sayers, R. Murray, J. Cunningham, A. Borbett.

West Stanley Schools District Team 1952 - 1953

Danny Fagan recalls: West Stanley Schools District team played Seaham Boys at Murray Park, Stanley in the final of the Durham County Associations Cup. They won 6-1, goals being scored by J. Robinson (4) and D. Fagan (2). Colin Milburn went on to be a top class cricketer playing for Northampton and England. He scored a century against a touring international side, when still a pupil at school. John Cunningham has become a 'local hero' for all of the good work he has done in raising money for charity.

West Stanley Schools District team. Back row, left to right: B Simpson (A. Plain), C. Milburn (Leazes), A. McArdle (A. Plain), C. Simpson (A. Plain), A. Jackson (Bloemfontein), D. McNeil (St Mary's). Front row: D. Fagan (St Joseph's), G. Dewey (T. Lea), I. Robinson (Front Street), J. Cunningham (Greenland), C. Henderson (T. Lea)

Stanley Schools' Football, 1969 by Pat McCue

The highlight of the Stanley Schools' FA history came in January 1969 when our small association, consisting of only six secondary schools, reached the open rounds of the English Schools U-15 Trophy for the only time. We were drawn away to Kirby Boys. Our immediate reaction was, 'Where is Kirby?' We discovered it was a new 'overspill' town, 15 miles from Liverpool, the setting for the TV series, 'Z Cars'. They had an awesome reputation, having previously reached the semi-final of this competition twice. In mid January we travelled down to Southport for an overnight stay; very much the underdogs. On the Saturday morning we moved over to Kirby Stadium where, in an intimidating atmosphere, our lads battled out a 2-2 draw, very much to the surprise of the home officials, who admitted later that they had anticipated an easy victory. The Stanley squad was as follows: Malcolm Brown, David Coxon, Alex Tait (Tanfield), Alan Scott, Jeff Hart, Joe Hillary, Andy Spencer, Colin Coulson (Annfield Plain Grammar Tech), Frank Tobin, Peter Kruk (St Bede's Lanchester), John Gray, John Swinburne (Shield Row), John Nichol (South Stanley), Gerard Proud and John Mallett (Towneley). The officials comprised: Syd Davies (secretary), Bob Symons (trainer), Derek Watson (chairman), Pat McCue, Danny Fagan, Alan Westwater (coaching staff). The Kirby team contained a centre back – Phil Thompson – later to captain Liverpool and England. A fortnight later the replay took place at the Morrison Busty Ground. The game attracted a 4,000 crowd and we were confident that we could finish Kirby off. On the day, however, our lads 'froze' and we were lucky to scramble a 1-1 draw. Under the rules of the competition we had to return to Kirby for a second replay. After a ding-dong struggle we went down 2-1 but gained the lasting respect of the Kirby association, who we played in friendly games the following year. Kirby, having beaten us after three games, went on to reach the semi-final of the competition. Happy memories!

Barry Venison

Barry Vennison, born 16th August 1964, joined Sunderland AFC straight from school as an apprentice aged 15. He made his league debut for Sunderland on 10th October 1981 and went on to make over 200 appearances for the Roker club, scoring three goals. Playing at both right back and midfield, he was made captain at only 19. In 1985 he led the Sunderland side out at Wembley for the League Cup Final, making him the youngest ever Cup Final captain. In July 1986 Barry was transferred to Liverpool, making his debut in the Charity Shield, one of five Charity Shield appearances. While at Anfield he made over 160 appearances, scoring once, and winning two League Championship winners' medals and one FA Cup winners' medals. Barry joined Newcastle United in July 1992 and captained the team to the First Division Championship in his first season. He played one season at right back, one season at centre half and one season in midfield, playing over 150 games, scoring one goal. He was transferred to Turkish

Barry with the FA Cup during his Liverpool days.

champions Galatasaray of Istanbul in the summer of 1995 and played as a sweeper or in midfield in over 20 games. Returning to the Premiership with Southampton late in 1995 for £1 million, he made over 30 appearances before undergoing two major back operations and was forced into early retirement in 1997.

International Honours.

Captain of England Under 18 team.
Captain of England Under 21 team – 10 caps.
Two Full England international caps against USA and Uruguay in 1994.

Ron Batty

This never say die defender, born in West Stanley, spent his schooldays at West Stanley Board School and Stanley Grammar. His first team was the Grammar School Inter House XI. He later signed for Quaking Houses Juniors and later East Tanfield. In 1943 he won winners medals for both NW Durham Junior League and the Junior Cup. After a spell with Spennymoor (NE League), he joined Newcastle United in 1945 and earned an FA Cup Winners' Medal in 1955.

Eric Larmour

Left: Ron Batty in the famous black and white stripes of Newcastle United.

West Stanley Amateur Swimming Club (ASC)

West Stanley Amateur Swimming Club (ASC) was formed in 1912 and held their galas at the old open air swimming pool that was situated some 100 yards south of Slaidburn Road, adjacent to the King's Head sports field.

The club had notable successes, with the Blackett family prominent in championship meetings. The club was finally forced to disband however in 1936, this being a sequel to the closure of West Stanley 'Burns' Colliery, which stood nearby. The swimming club had been dependent upon water pumped from the colliery to fill their pool.

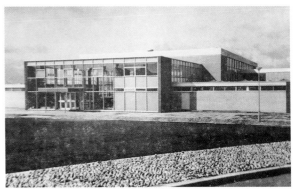

Plans were afoot to construct new bathing facilities and in 1939 a tender of £24,000 was awarded to Joesph Ayton and Sons of Blackhill. With architect fees and other expenses, the final cost was estimated at £28,000. The new facilities were to have a 190 foot frontage, a pool of 100 feet by 40 feet and water chute, spring board, full diving stage and accommodation for 500 bathers. In addition, a gym 60 feet by 40 feet would be provided together with a tea

The frontage of the newly constructed swimming baths, 1965.

room, kitchen and meeting room. The building was to be constructed opposite the Drill Hall and adjacent to the King's Head field.

Within a few months the onset of the Second World War caused the cancellation of the project. Subsequent approaches were made for funding in 1945, 1947, 1954 and 1955, but it was not until the opening of the swimming baths in August 1965 that a new generation of youngsters could compete for the newly reformed Stanley ASC. At a cost of £220,000 it heralded the end of Stanley Council's fight for an enclosed pool.

Following many years of competitive successes the club, the now Derwentside ASC, was again faced with disbandment when it was revealed that the relatively new facilities were deemed structurally unsafe. Despite much local disbelief and acrimony the swimming and sauna complex was hastily demolished in 1998. Derwentside Council is at present submitting plans to the National Lottery for funding for a new swimming complex to be built behind the Louisa sports centre.

A pristine pool awaiting the first bathers, 1965.

Northumberland and Durham swimming championships in 1983. Stanley ASC swimmers proudly display their trophies. Front: Philip Hindson. Second row, left to right: Julie King, Susan Bracegirdle and Allison Baker Third row: Jimmy Wilkinson, David Glendinning, and Richard Harrison. Back row: David McNulty, Kevin Burns, Adrian Hindson and Carol Ann Stanyer.

Below: The end of the affair – the baths almost totally demolished and rubble and scrap fill the once immaculate pool in 1998. The street in the background is Slaidburn Road. The old open air pool stood some 100 yards to the left of the houses.

South Moor Cricket Club

The first recorded match in a newspaper involving South Moor was against neighbouring Burnhope in 1885, with the latter team being victorious. The club had their first playing pitch at New Acres Farm, which still stands today at the top of Wilkinson's Bank on the South Moor to Burnhope Road. The club moved to their present ground, adjacent to Quaking Houses at the turn of the century. Original pavilions, comprising an empty outhouse, then a wooden shuttered structure, were superseded in 1910, when a brick pavilion was

South Moor Cricket Club – The pavilion in the 1970s.

opened on the west side of the ground. The club played its matches in the North West Durham League and were champions in each successive year from 1906 to 1911, and again in 1914. Matches were suspended from 1915-18 and following the war they again won the League in 1925, repeating the feat in 1928 and 1929. In 1934 the club joined the Tyneside Senior Cricket League and, eventually, in 1947 they won the championship for the first and only time. Seasons 1952-53 were played at King's Head Field owing to their ground and pavilion being repaired and renovated. The outfield was to be relevelled and a new turf square laid. Upon completion their first match back 'home' took place in April 1954. In 1974 a new club house and bar was officially opened, sited at the entrance to the ground. Dressing rooms were added in 1980 and in that same year the old pavilion, in a poor state of repair, was demolished.

South Moor Cricket Club, Tyneside Senior League Division A champions, 1947. Back row: W. Roxby, D. Langley (professional), J. Dalglish, M. Pounder, J.B. Errington, F. Hardy. Front row: S. Peart, W.T. Reynoldson, J. Dobson, J.G. Keeler, J. Cole.

South Moor 1st Eleven outside the pavilion, 1949. Back row: G. Storey, M. McVittie, A.R.J. Steward, S. Peart, R. Lumley, O. Barrass. Front row: P. Hughes, W.T. Reynoldson, H. Jordan, J. Gowland, D. Dodd.

The Hodgson Brothers

Craghead brothers Ted Hodgson (left) and Leo, receiving final instructions from referee George Harwood before a bout at Craghead Colliery Sports Day Carnival in 1951.

Leo started boxing in 1949 and received help from George Harwood, himself a former champion. Leo won the NCB Flyweight title at Washington Welfare Hall and boxed at national level until 1958. He had 169 fights losing only 9. Brother Ted won the NCB Featherweight title at Blackpool.

George Harwood

George Harwood

Born 31st July 1902, George Henry Harwood's first love was wrestling. However, he soon realised he was too light for the grappling game and switched to boxing, while working at the William Pit, Craghead.

In 1919 he won the amateur flyweight championship of Associated Gymnasia at Bradford with three knockouts and a points win over his opponents.

Married at 18, George took to the paid game in a big way in 1926, the year of the General Strike. He had five contests with Eddie Barrass, a grand little battler from Lanchester, winning four on points but having to capitulate in one fight retiring in the seventh round with a cut ear, in a tussle at South Moor in 1928.

Revenge was swift for George as two months later he defeated Eddie, again at South Moor, on points over 15 rounds. The referee on that occasion was non-other than Roland Todd, ex-middleweight champion of Great Britain. The match carried with it side stakes of £50, a considerable sum in those austere times. Throughout his career George Harwood was never knocked out but cut eyes caused him to retire several times.

View Lane Bowling Club, N.W. Durham League champions, 1956. Over the years, View Lane Bowls team have had some excellent players and the following team were no exception winning the league in 1956. The team included the following. Back row, left to right: T. Davison, T. Pearson, J. Wrightson, J. Peel, J. Boyle, G. Kay, M. Stafford, A. Urwin, T. Symonds. Middle row: J. Kennedy, F. Wilkinson, R. Siddle, G. Forster, G. Shield, A. York, J. McMichael, G. Alsop. Front row: O. Wilson, T. Paxton, J. Brown, J. Minto, J. Small, F. Boyle, H. Wright, G. Swinburne, W. Hair, J. Austin, R. Emmerson, R. Watt.

PEOPLE AND EVENTS

Ransome and Marles Bearing Factory's Children's Christmas Party, 1958. The factory opened at Greencroft in 1953 and was one of the area's biggest employers. It eventually closed in 1981.

Michael Heaviside V.C.

Born in 1880 in Gilesgate, Durham City, Michael and his family moved when he was a boy to Kimblesworth and later to Sacriston, where his father worked in the local pit.

On the death of his mother, Michael enlisted in the Royal Army Medical Corps and served in the Boer War.

He settled in Burnhope for a while working in the local colliery, now married, he later transferred to the Oswald Pit Craghead.

Upon the outbreak of the First World War, Michael re-enlisted and crossed to France in 1915. The battle of Arras began in April 1917 when the British Army attacked the German Hindenburg Line – a well-fortified system of trenches.

The 15th DLI, in which Michael was serving, were in the thick of things and German snipers and machine gunners were exacting a heavy toll on the British forces. On the afternoon of 6th May a sentry noticed movement in a shell hole some 40 yards from the German line.

The official account of Michael Heaviside's subsequent heroism states:

'When the battalion was holding a block in the line a wounded man was observed about 2pm in a shell hole some 60 yards in advance of our block and about 40 yards from the enemy line. He was making signals of distress and holding up an empty water bottle. Owing to snipers and machine gun fire it was impossible during daylight to send out a stretcher party. But Pte. Heaviside at once volunteered to carry water and food to the wounded man, despite enemy fire.

This he succeeded in doing and found the man to be badly wounded and nearly demented with thirst. He had lain out for 4 days and 3 nights and the arrival of the water undoubtedly saved his life.

Pte. Heaviside, who is a stretcher-bearer, succeeded the same evening, with the assistance of two comrades, in rescuing the wounded man.'

For this gallant action Michael was awarded the Victoria Cross and was duly presented with it by King George V at Buckingham Palace. A week earlier he has received a rapturous welcome when he had returned home on leave.

Following the war Heaviside V.C. returned to work as a miner at Craghead. In April 1939, aged 58, he died at his home in Bloemfontein Terrace. In July 1957 his V.C. and other medals were presented to the DLI Regimental Museum.

Stanley Central WMC, 1962. Back row, left to right: Doug Kendall, George Mitchell, Hugh McPhail, Ron Welch, Jim Freeman, Eddie Harwood, George Lyons. Middle: Jack Thirlaway, George Middlemass. Front row: Mary Thorp, George St Vincent Lee, Maureen Denton.

On 29th March 1980 Gilmonby House, which was originally a house and shop built in 1912 and known as Sloane's shop, was blown up by a gas explosion. The main road named Chester Road was for years troubled by subsidence due to former pit workings and consequently when a major gas leak occurred escaping gas travelled

through various cavities building up underneath the house. The property was owned by Joe Watson who, along with his family and a friend were in the house. No-one was killed, Raymond Slater was badly burnt and Mr Watson's mother who was 82 years of age was blown out of her invalid chair and suffered a broken ankle and a broken thigh. The house was next to the Northern Bus depot. The site is now occupied by a second hand car firm called Ash Motors.

South Moor Excelsior Club and Institute. Retirement of Steward, E. 'Ned' Frazer, 1923-55. Back row, left to right: W. Reay, T. Thompson, W. Foster, J. Renwick, W.G. Palmer, W. Nichols, R. Bell, R. Pilkington, R. Cook, W. Robson. Front row: R. Neal (chairman), C. Sloan, E. Frazer Jnr, E. Frazer Snr (steward), Mrs A. Frazer, R. Postle, H. Middlemast (treasurer), R. Green (secretary). Ned Frazer was also prominent in the fight game. A noted scrapper himself he also owned and promoted fights from his canvas topped boxing booth which stood at weekends behind the 'Ex' club. He found time to referee some bouts and also trained fighters – George Harwood being a prime example. 'Ned' had two good contests against Tim Mansell result 1-1. The first fight took place at St James', Newcastle. The second bout, at Craghead, was refereed by none other than Tommy Burns, former Heavyweight Champion of the World.

Shooting Gallery owned by Mr John Douglas of Stanley. Mr Douglas and his wife are holding rifles at their gallery, *circa* 1900.

RAF plane crash at Charlie Pit, 1941. Local policeman, Jim Harcus is second from the right in the backgound.

The Auxiliary Fire Service during the Second World War. The photograph was taken between shops at Bloemfontein. The street in the background is South View. Included in the picture: Mr Knox, Joseph Hall, Mr Traverse, Mr Pounder, Andrew Moore (chief).

Hollyhill Gardens Coronation Street Party. The children are pictured outside the house of Mrs Hall and Mrs Ward at 99 and 100 Hollyhill Gardens East. They had their Street Party at the Masonic Hall, Stanley to celebrate the Coronation of Queen Elizabeth II.

A group of Home Guard outside South Moor Colliery Offices. They include: Fred Barratt, Matty Williams, Edward Liddle, Ronnie Appleby, Alf Liddell, G. Lumley, G. Trow, Harold Gales, Jack Eccles, J. Williams, T. Walker, Les Watson, Fred Watson, Ralph Reed, T. Buckley, M. Cordy, Jack Allen, Jack Christopher, Percy Kelly, ? Glister, Tom Jennings, T. Baker, A. Clark, Bill Curry, H. Smart, J. Rutherford, E. Eagle, A. Thompson, W. Kay, Fred Temple, Dick Simms, Jack Wanless, Dick Webber, Jack Webber, Robson Porter, ? Barrass, W. Ward, N. Postle and many others, names not known. Most districts had their own units of volunteers formed as 'The Home Guard', assembled as a last line of defence against a German Invasion during the Second World War. In our area, they were mostly manned by miners and local trades people. These groups took their training very seriously, and would have, if called on, defended their country.

West Stanley campers during the 1926 General Strike.

1st South Moor (St George's) Scouts Gang Shows. Included in photograph: Jack Fenwick, Eddie Burrows, Jack Dawby, Dick Pearson, Keith Errington. The very first production in the South Moor Church Hall took place in 1950, a musical play produced by Dennis Buckley – Assistant Scoutmaster (Senior Scouts). The following year, for the very first time, the cast were allowed to wear the traditional Gang Show costumes of all white, a feature which is common to every Gang Show throughout the world. In 1953 the production saw a change from piano/drum accompaniment to an 8 piece orchestra and in 1958 a cast of 50 members provided entertainment for 6 nights. 1960 saw the final production in the Church Hall with the following year's show taking place in the newly constructed Civic Hall. The orchestra now numbered 11 with a cast of over 70. The final production for the group was in 1964.

Captain Benson's father, Thomas, qualified in 1870 as a surgeon and later a physician (colliery doctor). He set up practice in Ramsay Street with one house serving as a surgery and one house used as living quarters.

The family later moved to Stanley House (later the site of the Pavilion Cinema), then to Mayo House, Station Road; and finally, in 1924 to Causey Lodge which the family had specifically built for them and where Captain Benson's son, William Arthur Benson GP resides to this day.

Captain William Arthur Benson, 8th Battalion DLI (middle row, centre)

Captain Benson served in the First World War and finally retired from general practice in 1961 having been the senior partner in two different partnerships, first with Dr J. Charles and Dr A. Dewar and later with his son and Dr H.H. Morrison.

Louisa Wagon Shop (Louisa Pit), 1948. Back row, left to right: George Mitchell, John Davison, Tommy Robinson, George Sanders. Front row: Bill Davison, Jacky Kerr, Harry Hender.

The Victoria Club on Station Road was one of the best loved clubs of the area, but after falling on hard times, it was taken over by Tetley's and later resold and opened as the Hollywood. It changed hands yet again and traded as Tojos. This also failed and after standing empty for some time, vandals broke in and set fire to the building. The picture shows a view of the total destruction of this once fine club.

However, the structure remained sound and in the following years was transformed into apartments.

The Bombs At Beamish
By Jack Hair

Beamish is now world famous for its Open Air Museum and has thousands of visitors each year from Britain, Europe and beyond. On Friday 1st May 1942 at 2.55 am the only visitors there, were a German Bomb Crew seeking a target to offload their high explosive bombs. It was early morning and the sky was clear.

From above Beamish, the pilot would have seen the reflection from the two sets of railway lines, the LNER to Consett Steel Works and the Colliery coal line with the village of Beamish nestled in between. With the river nearby, it may have looked like a prime factory site. Whatever the reason, they dropped three high explosive bombs and then went off in search of other targets.

It was later said that Beamish was bombed solely because of the so called Miracle of Durham when the German bombers were unable to find the City of Durham due to a cloud of mist that arose from the river totally engulfing the city. It was also supposed to be part of the Baedecker raids and that this particular raid had been foiled by British Intelligence who had cracked the German codes and also perfected a system whereby they could block out the German electronic target signalling device throwing them way off target drawing the bombers away from the cities. If this was so, then Durham's miracle became Beamish's nightmare.

Red Alert had been sounded at Blaydon at 2.33 am and the area had all been warned of an impending air raid by siren alarms. People throughout the area were by now in their air raid shelters or under the stairs of their homes, which was a regular place to hide. At 2.55 am one of the bombs at Beamish exploded on impact causing damage to some of the shops and houses. A second bomb was found shortly afterwards on the embankment of the colliery railway line beside a wooden footbridge and dangerously close to shops and houses. Local people were evacuated.

At approximately 9.30 am a Bomb Disposal bomb was approaching Beamish when they were held up at a railway crossing to allow a train to pass. Just after the train passed they heard a loud explosion up in the village. The area of the shops and houses near the Post Office had been cleared and roped off. Had it not been for the delay at the crossing, the bomb squad would probably have been killed by the explosion of this second bomb. Part of the railway line was uprooted and foot bridge was badly damaged. A water main was fractured and there was further damage to the nearby shops and houses.

All that day, there was great interest in these explosions with many people travelling from the surrounding areas to satisfy their curiosity. None of them was aware of a third bomb lying unexploded in a

Station Road, Beamish.

nearby shop, with its clockwork timer slowly ticking away. This bomb had gone through the roof of the building leaving only a very small hole. Geoff Anderson who lived in an apartment above Smith's shop, said that when he had been allowed back into his flat later, he looked in his cupboard for his slippers only to find there was no floor in the cupboard. The bomb had obviously gone straight through into the shop below and was lying there, ticking away.

At 9.05 pm that night, people were waiting at the bus stop opposite the shops for their bus home. Children were playing in the street and Special Constable Sam Edgell was nearby. Suddenly, an explosion ripped across the road toward the bus stop and the waiting crowd. Trees were blown down. Stones, glass and people were hurled into the air. Villagers rushed from their homes to the scene only to be greeted by a cloud of dust and smoke, temporarily hiding the horrendous scene. When the dust settled, they could not believe their eyes. Twisted bodies lay all around and the injured lay among the dead, too stunned even to cry out.

Jack Edgell had rushed from his home in Woodside knowing his father was on duty. The first casualty he came across was his father Sam, unconscious, badly injured, but still alive. Jack noticed his father had no boots on. They had been blown off his feet in the blast. Women sobbed openly and tears ran down the faces of the burly miners as they found two tiny bodies. One was Clive Lawson aged 9, the grandson of MP Jack Lawson from 7, Woodside, Beamish. The other was 8-year-old Irene Seymour from School Terrace, South Moor. She had been with her grandmother, Matilda Seymour aged 77 who lay nearby, badly injured.

The casualties were checked one by one. Mrs Palmer had broken her shoulder. Audrey Lumley, Dodie Dobson, Alec Walker, Mrs Barker and many others were hurt. Gwendolen Hannant aged 17 of Delacour Street, Stanley was found dead. Ten-year-old Sylvia Spence of Bloemfontein was found severely injured close to her mother, Elizabeth Spence who also had terrible injuries. The body of Special Constable Robert Reay aged 61 of Urpeth Hilltop was found in the damaged building. He had been helping with repairs to the shops. The dead and injured were carried to Pit Hill Farmhouse. The less seriously injured were treated on the spot. The more seriously injured were taken to the

Beamish Station.

Emergency Hospital at Chester-le-Street, and some of these were sent on to specialist hospitals. Mrs Spence and Mrs Seymour died next day and by Monday the death toll had risen to 8 with the deaths of Sylvia Spence and Sam Edgell. Seven were seriously injured with approximately 28 others injured.

It is also worth noting that on that fateful day, Margaret Duffy of Stanley had been visiting her brother Arthur Dempster at his home in Wallsend when they also died with others due to enemy bombing at Wallsend.

The funerals took place over the next few days after the explosion and little information of the disaster was mentioned in the papers at that time. It was a question of security.

Extracts from statements from some of those involved in the explosion.
I was 13 years old and can remember standing with my family at the bus stop but have no recollection of the explosion. My first memory after was of waking up in Chester-le-Street Hospital. I lost a finger on my left hand and had severe head injuries. I also had leg injuries and still have a piece of shrapnel in my leg. I was in hospital for a month and so ill at one time that my father was sent for. I knew nothing of my sister or mother's deaths until I went home.

Joyce Spence

Ethel can't talk very well but she was badly injured with her left ankle almost severed. She had many injuries and was in hospital until the following September.

Ethel Spence

We walked as a family to Beamish that day to visit a family friend to check that he was all right. I was a short distance away from the bus stop with my sister Violet when the bomb went off. The scene was terrible and when the dust settled we tried to get through to the rest of the family but were held back. I later saw them at the farmhouse nearby where the family were taken. My mother was almost unrecognisable and only identified by my father the next day by her broad wedding ring. My father died within one year of this disaster, it was said of a broken heart.

Elizabeth Spence

My mother, sister Betty and myself had walked down from Greencroft to my grandparents at Bloemfontein where we met our relatives, the Spence's. We all then walked down to Beamish to see the Walker family. After visiting, I was standing at the bus stop but have no memory of the explosion. My first memory was of lying on the ground saying, 'My shoe is missing'. I was taken with the others to the farmhouse and as I lay on this table with my legs dangling over, my aunt, Mrs Spence lay below, unconscious, with serious head wounds. I was 12 at the time and my sister Betty was ten.

Ivy Riley

I had only recently began going out with Gwen Hannet and that particular day we had gone down to Beamish to see if Gwen's friend, Audrey Lumley and her family were alright following the first explosions. At that time, I had my call up papers to go into the RAF in my pocket. After looking around we stood chatting outside Lumley's shop waiting for the bus. The next thing I recall was lying totally covered by rubble bricks and debris. It felt as though stone dust completely filled my body. I was trapped by my body and legs but managed to free my head. I heard some voices say, 'There's another one here'. As they began to free me I remember saying, 'There's someone else beneath my feet, get her out'. The three men who found me were Craghead Colliery deputies, Bob Abbott, Matt Davidson and Matt Young. They had arrived at the scene just as the bomb had exploded. After treatment I was transferred to Winterton

Hospital with serious leg injuries and stayed there for several months. After that I was called into the RAF.

James R. Healey

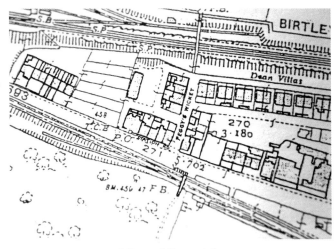

Map of Beamish.

I was 9 years old at the time and had been staying at South Urpeth Farm with my sister, Elsie. I was travelling back home to Stanley accompanied by Ella Coyle, Tommy Coyle, Tommy Weatherspoon, and Les Dodd. The buses were crowded so we decided to walk. When reaching Beamish Village, we decided to have a look around and were in the area of Peggy's Wicket when the bomb exploded only yards from where Tommy and I stood. Tommy had injuries to his left hand and I had three evenly spaced cuts on my head. The shoe laces had been blown out of my shoes and all the buttons on our clothes had also been blown off. After treatment, I was taken back to the farm where that night we listened to Lord Haw Haw on the radio saying that German bombers had bombed the Rail Junction Yards at Twizel.

Syd Wears

I lived with my aunts in the shop at Station Road, Beamish. We were awakened by the air raid sirens through the night. I was 18 at the time. The first bomb brought window shutters down in the house. We were evacuated from the house and shop by the ARP Warden to the shelter at the back of the property. the second bomb exploded at 9.00 am and the front of the buildings were badly damaged. People worked most of that day repairing the buildings. When Owen and Jim came down, we went off for a walk and later returned to the shop where we waited for their bus. I saw the bus coming up from Beamish Club. My next recollection was in hospital. I had head injuries and shock. My aunt had been blown into the sitting room by the blast but was uninjured and was rescued by some miners. Jack Draper later told us he had seen the hole in the roof and was convinced there was a third bomb but nobody would listen to him. Audrey on reflection believes she felt the shudder of that bomb as it came through the roof next door.

Audrey Lumley

On that day, my aunt and I were visiting the Lawsons. Clive took me to see the bomb damage and we played on the rubble until it was time to leave. My aunt and I were walking back to West Pelton and as we passed the saw mill there was a bang and a black cloud lifted over Beamish. We met my dad who was an ARP Warden. It was he and Sam Young who found the second bomb on the railway line earlier that day. My Dad went up to Beamish where he and Sam helped in the rescue. Sam pulled Audrey Lumley (Draper) from the rubble. Sadly my friend Clive Lawson with who I had just been playing was found dead.

A.W. Grindle

There are many other eye witness accounts of this disaster, sadly, too many to list in this brief account, but never the less equally significant

Parade to Craghead War Memorial. Craghead is well renowned for Remembrance Parades through the village and up to the splendid War Memorial. The parade shown took place on 7th November 1957 with representatives from the whole community taking part. The procession is just about to reach the war Memorial set in its own grounds.

Remembrance Day Service, also on 7th November 1957, the people of Craghead honoured those who gave their lives for their country at a service at the War Memorial. This memorial was first unveiled at a ceremony in the Memorial Grounds on 11th November 1922 at 2 pm  when the chairman, Mr Henry Greener welcomed at the gates, speakers, representatives and the general public. Mr T.Y. Greener officially opened the gates to the Memorial Ground.

Services still take place at Craghead Memorial Ground but on a much smaller scale than that shown in the photograph.

A Remembrance Service in the 1990s at Craghead showing Father David Beater conducting the service at the memorial.

Frederick John Wade 1886-1978

We are lucky in our area to have had several accomplished local historians including Ralph Powton, W. Jennings and the most prolific writer of them all, Fred Wade. Between them, they have left us with an accurate record of our past giving future historians a solid base from which to work. Fred's record as a local historian is respected throughout the county. Many of his books are used in the local libraries as a resource facility. Fred was born in Yorkshire, the son of John James and Jane Wade. His father was a joiner/cartwright and the family moved into South Moor when Fred was very young. He was educated at the National School on Wagtail Lane, and at 12 years of age became an apprentice mechanic at the Hedley Colliery, Old South Moor.

Frederick John Wade

He attended evening classes to better himself. Before the First World War, he was appointed assistant Enginewright at the Charlie Pit. Fred was a member of Stanley Territorials and went to France with the 8th Battalion DLI before transferring into the 151 Machine Gun Company. He served in France for 3 years before being wounded at Hill 60 near Ypres. In 1922 he was appointed Enginewright at the Morrison Busty Colliery where he remained until he retired in 1951. He had many interests and the following are but a few. He was Founder member of Annfield Plain & Stanley Naturalists, a member of Consett & the Vale of Derwent Naturalists, the Northern Naturalists Union, the Ramblers Association, the Fellowship of Fellworkers, and a member of the Machine Gun Corps Comrades Association. During his life, Fred gave many talks on local history and regularly wrote articles on this subject for the local newspapers. After retirement, he began to write his books all based on the local history and customs of our area. He was a widower for many years and had three sons and two daughters.

Oswald Barrass

Many people are well known for some specific event in their lives. However, it would be difficult to decide for which part of his life Ossie is best remembered, so varied are his attributes. To name but a few: teaching, cricket, football, the RAF, quiz leagues, local history, refereeing, umpiring and coaching; reaching a high standard in all. Born in Elm Street, South Moor in 1927, he attended South Moor Infants, Greenland School and then Alderman Wood Grammar School (Tanfield). He then qualified as a teacher at the age of 19 at Sheffield. His first teaching post was at Pelton Roseberry Boys School before serving in the RAF 1946-49. He returned to teaching in 1949 at Craghead County School and remained there until 1964. While at this school he went

Oswald Barrass

back to College at Durham to gain higher qualification in teaching. In 1961 he was appointed Deputy Head at Craghead. In 1964, he was appointed Head Teacher at South Moor Greenland School and remained there until he retired in 1984. During his years in education he was at the forefront of raising standards in schools particularly at mathematics. Ossie played cricket and football for a host of different clubs. He also coached cricket and football at the schools he taught at with great success at both sports. During his sporting life Ossie qualified as a football referee and cricket umpire and since retiring from active sport, he has umpired in the Tyneside Senior League, Durham University, Durham County Under 19s Cup competitions and Durham 1st XI against Scotland (rained off) and is still on the TSL Umpire list at 71. While in the RAF Ossie trained as an aircraft wireless mechanic attached to a squadron of Vampire jets at Odsham with Squadron 54, 72 and 247. He married Doris (née Robinson) in 1953 and has daughters Susan and Helen. Apart from taking part in sport, he has also acted as an official for many organisations particularly South Moor Cricket Club, Stanley RAFA, Stanley Past & Present History Group and many other organisations too numerous to mention. As a teacher, coach of young people, sportsman, referee and umpire, plus many other things, Ossie has served this area with great distinction and will be remembered in the future by so many for his great contribution to sport and the community of which he is so proud.

Some members of Oxhill Youth Club on a day trip to Marsden in the 1950s. Included are: Girls, N. Jeans, J. Batty, I. Meek, J. Armstrong, M. Ruddick; Boys, J. Daglish, J. Kerr, A. Fawcett, A. Peart, M. Pickard.

The Last Train to Consett

Engine 92066 is shown going through Stanley on its way up to Consett filled with rail enthusiasts for the last time on Saturday 17th March 1984. This train was chartered by the Derwentside Rail Action Group to mark the loss of the 150 year old line. This photograph was taken by Ivan Garnham.

A line from Stanhope to Annfield Plain opened 15th March 1834 and a section through Stanley to Washington opened on 1st September the same year. Sadly, the Stanhope Limeworks went bankrupt in 1839 and the line closed down. It was taken over on the western section by Derwent Iron Co and on the eastern section by the Pontop & South Shields Railway Co under the guidance of Robert Stephenson. By around 1844 the line was taken over by railway king, George Hudson as part of Newcastle & Darlington Traction Railway, a pre-runner of NER.

There were great improvements between 1856-1893. Old inclines were bypassed at Annfield Hill in 1882 and between Stanley and Pelaw via Beamish, an eight mile stretch in 1887. In 1896 the route was opened to passengers and closed to passengers on 23rd May 1955. The line remained open to freight until 1983. After the last journey in 1984, the rails were removed and re-laid at Great Ayton on the Whitby line.

Right: An old steam train on its way to Consett. The LNER line through Stanley was used mostly for iron ore to the steelworks and coal from local collieries. Passenger trains never really caught on commercially.

Hillary Rodham Clinton – From Kip Hill To The White House
By Jack Hair

The Durham miner was a special breed of man, versatile, hard working, loyal and capable of adapting to any challenge. The men and their families had travelled into the area for work and if ever the work ran out or problems prevented them from progressing, they would think nothing of taking up the challenge and moving to other areas of employment. The houses they had lived in were owned by the coal owners so it was easy to just pick up and go. In the late 19th century, many were tempted to try their luck in the New World of America and the Rodhams of Oxhill were such a family.

Jonathan Rodham had reached the position of Overman in the local colliery which was just about as high a position as a working man could go in this industry. Who knows what his reasons were, but in 1883, he and his family left Durham to travel to

Hillary Rodham Clinton

the USA. Just over one hundred years later, his great granddaughter became the First Lady of America, wife of the President of the USA – Hillary Rodham Clinton.

The following is a brief account of the Rodhams in Durham and in particular, the district of Stanley in North Durham.

To tell this story, we go back to May 1774 when Joseph Rodham married Dorothy Bell at Chester-le-Street Parish Church. After marrying, the next entry is of their son Jonathan being baptised at Washington in June 1775. At this time they lived at Black Fell, Washington but soon moved into the Birtley area from where their next children were born. John 1776, Ann 1778, second son Jonathan 1779, Dorothy 1781, twins Joseph and Mary 1784 and John 1787. Jonathan and John both died in infancy and were buried together at Chester-le-Street in 1777. The second son named John died at North Thorn, Shield Row, Stanley and was buried at Tanfield in 1789. The remaining five children survived infancy. It was around 1779 when the family moved from Birtley to Shield Row and Joseph began work in the local colliery.

Joseph died at North Thorn in 1822 aged 80. His wife Dorothy died at North Thorn in 1835 aged 87. They were both buried at Tanfield. Their son Jonathan, born in 1779 is the next line of interest. He was also a coal miner at Shield Row. In 1804, aged 24, he married Margaret Orange aged 20 at St Margaret's Church, Tanfield. after their marriage they continued to live at North Thorn and in December 1804, son Thomas was born. Sadly, Margaret died in February 1805 and was buried at

Map of Craghead.

CERTIFIED COPY of an   ENTRY OF BIRTH
Pursuant to the Births and   Deaths Registration Act 1953

Registration District   Lanchester

1843. Birth in the Sub-district of _Lanchester_ in the _County of Durham_

No.	When and where born	Name, if any	Sex	Name and surname of father	Name, surname and maiden surname of mother	Occupation of father	Signature, description, and residence of informant	When registered
40	Seventh June 1843 at Waglaid Cottages in the Township of Holmside	Jonathan	Boy	Joseph Rodham	Elizabeth Rodham formerly Scurfield	Coal Mine	Elizabeth x Rodham her mark Mother Waglaid Cottages	Fourteenth of June 1843

Certified to be a true copy of an entry in a register in my custody.

Patricia Garland

CAUTION:—It is an offence to falsify a certificate or to make or knowingly use a false certificate or a copy of a false certificate intending it to be accepted as genuine to the prejudice of any person, or to possess a certificate knowing it to be false without lawful authority.

WARNING: THIS CERTIFICATE IS NOT EVIDENCE OF THE IDENTITY OF THE PERSON PRESENTING IT.

Jonathan Rodham's Birth Certificate.

Tanfield. In those early years, the area of North Thorn was situated between what we now know as the lower end of Shield Row and Barn Hill on the north side of Shield Row Bank.

In November 1805, Jonathan married his second wife, Ann Parkinson at Durham City and they went on to have nine children. Dorothy at North Thorn 1806, William at South Moor 1810, Joseph at South Moor 1812. (The South Moor mentioned was likely to be an area of land between Shield Row and Oxhill and not the area we now know as South Moor.) Jonathan and Ann then moved to Quarry House near Oxhill. Mary was born 1814, Joseph died 1815 and a second son Joseph was born in 1817 also at Quarry House. They had a daughter named Ann. In 1819, Mary died. John was born in 1821 and the family then moved to Kip Hill. Their last child Ralph was born there in November 1824.

Jonathan's wife Ann died in 1836 and was buried at Tanfield.

The next line is Joseph, born in 1817. He, like his father Jonathan, was also a miner and for a time worked at Shield Row Colliery. In 1839-40, he moved to Craghead to the newly opened William Pit owned by Hedley. He married Elizabeth Scurfield of Craghead in 1840. They had seven children of which five

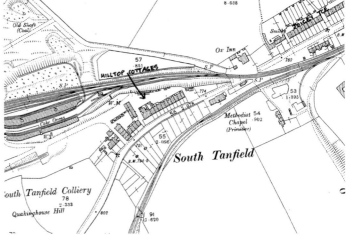

Map of Oxhill.

were born at Craghead in 1840. Their names and years born are as follows: Margaret 1842, Jonathan 1843, Mary Ann 1846, Thomas 1848, Elizabeth 1850, Dorothy 1854, and Isabella 1859. Joseph later moved to South Pontop Colliery in Collierley Parish (Hare Law).

The next in the tree is Jonathan Rodham, born in 1843. While working at South Pontop Colliery, he married Isabella Simpson Bell at St Thomas's Church, Harelaw on New Year's Eve 1867. He eventually reached the position of Colliery Overman. They had the following children in the Stanley District: Thomas Bell 1868 at Greencroft, Elizabeth 1869 at Oxhill, Margaret 1871 at Kyo, Isabella Simpson 1873 at Oxhill, Joseph 1874 at Oxhill, William Robert 1876 at Oxhill, Jonathan 1878 at Oxhill, Hugh 1879 at Oxhill, and Elizabeth 1881 at Annfield Plain. During this time, the family had moved colliery and house several times and for several years lived at Joicey Terrace, Oxhill.

When Baptized.	Child's Christian Name.	Parents' Name.		Abode.	Quality, Trade, or Profession.	By whom the Ceremony was performed.
		Christian.	Surname.			
1879 Oct 8th	Hugh	Jonathan & Isabella Simpson	Rodham, &c.	Hilltop	Overman	Thomas Hill Curate
No. 2020						

BAPTISMS solemnized in the Parish of Collierley in the County of Durham in the Year 1879

Hugh Rodham's Birth Certificate.

At least four of the children very probably attended Oxhill School. Their last address in County Durham was at 20 Hilltop Cottages, Oxhill in 1883 at which point Jonathan and his family emigrated to America finally settling in Pennsylvania. It is believed they had a further four children all born in America.

The next in line is Hugh Rodham, born in Oxhill in 1879. Hugh married Hannah Jones and they had three children one of which was Hugh Ellsworth Rodham born in 1912. In 1942, he married Dorothy Howell and their eldest of three children is Hillary Rodham who later married Bill Clinton, President of the United States of America. It is probably the fact she kept the name Rodham as part of her married name that drew attention in England to the fact that she was one of the Durham Rodhams, although in fairness, her biographer Donny Radcliffe had already picked this fact up in his book *A First Lady For Our Time* for Warner Books 1993. Hugh Rodham, born in Oxhill, Stanley, County Durham in 1879, the grandfather of Hillary Rodham Clinton, died in America in 1965.

Much of the above information was obtained from a paper by Geoff Nicholson of Washington, Tyne & Wear.

At the time of writing in 1999, there are still Rodhams directly related living in the Stanley area and many other relatives and if Hillary ever visits Stanley she can be assured of a great welcome.

A Disaster Waiting To Happen: The Louisa Morrison Colliery Disaster 1947
By Jack Hair

Just after the Second World War, there was a tremendous need for coal to regenerate our industries and the North East miners rose to this challenge, often working seven days a week. The coal mines were nationalised in January 1947 and a group of mines formerly owned by the South Moor Coal Co namely, the Louisa – the Morrison North and the William worked

Morrison Colliery with St Aidan's Church on the right.

between them the Middle Series of Durham seams. These were the Maudlin – Low Main and Hutton. These mines had a centrally situated upcast shaft. The Louisa Colliery was served by three downcast shafts, the Louisa, the Morrison North and the William. In 1947, between them they employed 1,480 men underground and 350 surface workers. There was a daily output of 1,450 tons most of which was wound up at the Louisa.

These three collieries worked between them the 4th North District which had a history of flooding and in 1947 had only recently been re-opened. Nearby there was a section of the Low Main where there had been a fire in 1929 which was still burning with the fire held back at that time by a brick wall. For a time this area was classed as a safety lamp area, while the Morrison North had been classed as a non-gassy pit (open light). This caused some concern to the union as miners were travelling to this district underground from three different downcast shafts with different categories of safety. The management agreed all men in that district would come under Louisa management and also the Louisa Miners Lodge. The total area then becoming worked by safety lamp and classed as a gassy area.

On the night of the disaster, 24 men had come back to do progress work and tidy up in the 4th North District. In the previous hours, Deputies and Overmen had tested for firedamp with none being found. Even 15 minutes before the explosion conditions were described as normal although Ted Errington who was in the area only minutes before the explosion described conditions as incredibly hot and humid with poor quality air. It was noted that none of the men carried flame gas detectors even though this was a colliery regulation. All they carried was their Eddison J. Electric lamps. Deputy Estell carried a flame safety lamp. The lampman was aware of this but said his job was only to hand out what was requested.

At 7 pm drillers Johnson and Kilgallon descended from the Louisa with the rest of the men descending from the Morrison North over the next few hours Deputies Hebden and Estell did their handover at the surface leaving the men unsupervised for a short while. Deputy Estell reached the district only moments before the explosion. At 11.55 pm there was an explosion in the 4th North District which resulted in the death of 22 miners.

The official cause of the explosion was as follows:

'An emission of firedamp from the strata below the Hutton Seam created an inflammable mixture of firedamp and air on the East Gate Line and the Straight East Gate. That shortly before midnight, a Lucifer Match was struck about the Loading Point on the Straight East Gate for the purpose of lighting a cigarette. This ignited the mixture and initiated a very mild firedamp explosion which developed additional force as it progressed and which was propagated by coal dust along the mechanical roadways both existing and disused throughout the district, and that the explosion was finally extinguished by the stone dust on the South Heading of the Main Drift.'

A Description of the Explosion
Just as Deputy Estell arrived at the 4th North District, there was an explosion. Nearby, three deputies were doing normal safety work at the point where the brick wall was holding back the fire which started in 1929. They were Younger, Shanley and Robinson. Younger looked at his watch and it was 11.55 pm. They felt a momentary stop of the intake air followed by a rush of dust from the Morrison North Shaft. It was obvious to them there had been an explosion.

These three men, were joined by Overman Hutchinson, and between them they carried out an act of great bravery never ever considering their own safety. In horrific conditions, with visibility down to two feet, and the air foul with poisonous gas and the area still on fire, they worked ceaselessly searching in the darkness for signs of life. Due to their heroic efforts, five men were brought out alive. They were Minto, Bailey, Johnson, Kilgallon and Deputy Estell. They also brought out many of the dead before they were joined by rescue teams. The survivors and the dead were brought up at the Morrison North where they were examined by Doctors Fox and Josephs. The injured were taken to Newcastle Infirmary while the dead were placed in a temporary mortuary in the Morrison. Sadly, Bailey died within 24 hours and Estell died the following day. After three months, Minto also died of his injuries. The two survivors Johnson and Kilgallon never really recovered from their ordeal.

The King Decorates Durham Pit Heroes
At the inquest, the Coroner publicly praised the heroism of the four men – Deputies Harry Robinson, Joseph Shanley and William Younger and Overman J. Hutchinson. They were later called to Buckingham Palace when they were decorated with the Edward Medal from King George VI. The medal was for their rescue efforts under conditions that would have tested the courage and endurance of the bravest and the strongest. The four rescue men also received the Carnegie Award for bravery at Stanley Court Office.

The Disaster Fund
On hearing of the disaster, Council Chairman Ed Farbridge immediately started a Disaster Fund appeal and by 31st March 1948 they had raised a total of £25,008 7s 3d. The Fund was planned to last for 20 years and there were 19 widows and 34 dependant children. The Fund lasted 20 years as planned.

The Four Lucky Blacksmiths
On the night of Friday 22nd August 1947, four blacksmiths from the Louisa were sent to the 4th North District to fit a girder. On arrival they could not find the girder and were directed back to bank. On the way out they passed several of the miners who were later killed. On reaching bank they walked back down the line to the Louisa Depot only to be told of the explosion and how it had been thought they were among the dead. The four blacksmiths were: Ted Errington, J. Cook, W. Joblin and T. Robinson.

The Bevin Boys

During and just after the war, some 45,000 eighteen-year-olds were conscripted into the Bevin Boys to serve their National Service down the coal mines. The group shown in the photograph served their training at the Morrison Colliery in 1944. Included in those killed in the Morrison Disaster were two

A group of Bevin Boys and staff at Morrison.

Bevin Boys, Francis E. Martin of Catchgate and Gerald Moore of Chichester. They both died in the service of their country, but to date have received no military recognition.

Conclusions

Not being a miner myself, my conclusions are taken only from the facts available at the time of my research. It would be wrong of me to try to persuade others that my thoughts are in any way meant to be considered as an official document. My conclusions are more in the way of questions to which I have no answers. I can only assume the official reasons were put forward due to lack of any other explanation.

1. There appears to have been an unsatisfactory arrangement of the single cloth across the outer end of Straight End Gate on the short length separating the intake air and the return air at this vital point. Mines Inspector Yates said that 'the single cloth was bad practice and not in compliance with the regulations'. In plain language illegal single cloth.

2. Undetected firedamp. There were no gas detector lamps in this area at the time of the explosion even though such lamps were compulsory under colliery regulations. The lampman was aware of this as was Deputy Hebden. Surely someone should have taken on this responsibility.

3. Coal dust in excess. The inspector pointed out that there were many areas, used and unused that were thick with coal dust which was against colliery procedure and that the said dust was responsible for the explosion growing from a small explosion into a disaster. The spreading of the explosion was solely due to the coal dust.

4. Cigarettes and matches. The miners had been supposedly searched for matches and cigarettes on the way into the pit yet a search of the bodies revealed several of the miners had both cigarettes and matches. The Mines

Inspector found clear evidence that smoking in the 4th North District had been taking place on a regular basis particularly at the Deputies' Kist where numerous cigarette ends and spent matches were found. This indicated that smoking had taken place over a long period probably in the knowledge of the management, even though this area had been identified as a safety lamp area. Smoking had still taken place against colliery regulations but in the knowledge of at least some of the management team.

Well, there seems no doubt that an illegal match was struck and that this indeed caused the initial explosion. However, had the colliery been run to regulation in connection with safety doors, safety lamps, coal dust build up and not allowing some of the men to smoke, then this would very probably have been a much smaller explosion with considerably less loss of life. However, as I said, it is only fair that you come to your own conclusions.

The 50th Anniversary, 23rd August 1997.

A Fund organised by Jack Hair helped by Rev Geoff Lawes, Ron Hindhaugh and Terry Fenwick paid for a Memorial Stone to be laid in St Aidan's Church grounds, almost opposite the Morrison Colliery gates, on 23rd August 1997. There was a Memorial Service held in the church with over three hundred in attendance, led by the former Bishop of Durham, the Rt Rev David Jenkins assisted by clergy from local churches. Also in attendance were the Annfield Plain Gleemen Male Voice Choir and Langley Park Colliery Band. Many relatives of those killed in the disaster attended and this was followed by a dedication service for the memorial stone in the church grounds. It was a very moving and sad day for most of those who attended but all seemed grateful that those killed had finally been remembered.

The Memorial Service at St Aidan's Church led by Bishop David Jenkins.

Chris Armstrong pictured with his drums in the Hibernian Hall. He was born at Office Row next to Burnhope Pit. He used to light the boilers at the Pit. After many years, he became winder man at Burnhope and at Beamish Mary. At one time or another, Chris has played the drums for most of the colliery bands in the area. His other great love was on the drums in local dance bands and entertaining in local clubs.

Below: Coronation Party, New Kyo, 1953. Included are: Jean Waddle, Ralph Wilson, Linda Brown, Norman Davison, Dorothy Wilson, Margaret Reardon, Marion Messenger, Ken Dunn, Margaret Pringle, Harriet Sandbell, Billy Wilson.

Stanley Groups by Ray Soulsby

In 1959 teenagers Raymond Soulsby and Terry Lewins were in a skiffle group, both playing guitar and singing. Later Raymond went on to play the tea chest bass. This was a brush shank fixed to the back of a chest. The top of the brush shank would have a piece of thick cord tied to it with the other end of the cord fixed to the tea chest. This was used as a cheap version of a double bass. An old wash board took the place of drums as no-one could afford a set of drums in those days. The wash board player would have thimbles on his fingers and would rub them over the corrugations and this would give a rhythm sound of its own.

ANNFIELD PLAIN A.F.C.

GRAND DANCE

THE CIVIC HALL, STANLEY

FRIDAY, 2nd AUGUST, 1963

9 p.m. till 2 a.m.

The North's Top Variety Group,

LIEL and THE SOLITAIRES

Light Refreshments.   Licensed Buffet until 1.0 a.m.
Late Transport.   ADMISSION **5/-**

Admission ticket for the Solitaires from 1963.

Raymond and Terry met Jack Hair, who had a good knowledge of stage presentation and who was himself a good ballad singer, and the three went around doing local charity shows. Jack told Raymond and Terry to move on and form what was coming popular – a rock group. By chance, at that time, two other teenagers were looking to form a rock group, they were Ian Herron and George Wilkinson.

The line up was Ian Herron – lead guitar, Terry Lewins – rhythm guitar,

The Solitaires, left to right: Ian Herron, Terry Lewins, Lyle Edwards, Ray Soulsby, George Wilkinson.

Raymond Soulsby – bass guitar and George Wilkinson – drums. All four were from the Stanley area. They looked for a lead singer and met up with Lyle Edwards from Ebchester. This was the original Solitiares.

The Premiers, left to right: Peter Urwin, Raymond Soulsby, Ronney Jobson. Front: John McPhail. Not on the photograph is the organist Gordon Dews.

Six months of rehearsals at the Hibernian Club at Stanley followed. This allowed the boys to keep up with the hits of the day as well as some of the old standards.

The first bookings were for charity shows, one of the best at that time was a show that would bring regular bookings. This was Friends of the Hospital, organised by local barber, Hughey McPhail. Local clubs in the Stanley area would have the show on at regular intervals. Other artists who appeared were: Eddie Harwood, Peter Donneley, George Lyons and Jimmy Freeman. All proceeds would go to local hospitals.

The Solitaires went on to play in clubs and dance halls all over the North East. They entered the 'Top Group of the North East Competition'. The Final was at the City Hall in Newcastle and The Solitiares came third out of around seventy groups that entered.

1. Sixteen Strings 121 marks.
2. Silver Dollars 115 marks.
3. The Solitiares 114 marks.

In order to go professional the group later reformed and were renamed The Geordies. They went on to play in London, Germany and Spain before breaking up in 1966.

Another group in the Stanley area was The Premiers: Ronney Jobson – lead guitar, Peter Urwin – drums, Raymond Soulsby – bass guitar, John McPhail – lead singer, Gordon Dews – organist. They also did lots of local charity shows and worked lots of the clubs in the North East. The Premiers were best known for their regular booking on a Friday night at the Arch Club.

The local music scene also produced the trio Triangle: Hunter Selkirk – lead guitar, John McPhail – lead singer and Raymond Soulsby – bass guitar.

Triangle, left to right: Hunter Selkirk, John McPhail, Raymond Soulsby.